REFLECTI   ᴎ THE TIMES AND LIFE OF WILLIAM 'BILL' ROACHE ACTOR FOR THE AGES

Rob Goodfellow • Jonathan Copeland • Peter O'Neill

timesandlife.co.uk

atebol
publishing

Published in Aotearoa New Zealand
by The End Authority Limited
The End Publishing Ltd
68 New North Road, Eden Terrace, Auckland 1021
Aotearoa New Zealand
publishing@theend.co.nz
theend.pub

Published in the UK all other jurisdictions by Atebol,
Adeiladau'r Fagwyr, Llandre, Aberystwyth, SY24 5AQ.
publishing@atebol.com
atebol.com

ISBN: 978-1-80106-283-1

For sisters Lottie and Jane Graham
Born in Kirkham (1884) and Salford (1886)
Verity and Will Roache and Rupert and Nicolas Pullee
and Rob Goodfellow's
Lancashire great-grandmothers
—who lived to love *Corrie*

Readers will soon discover that the commissioned ranks of the Royal Welch Fusiliers have included many great actors: Andrew Cruikshank (Major), Jack Hawkins (Lieutenant-Colonel), John Kidd (Captain), Desmond Llewellyn (Second-Lieutenant), André Morell (Major) and Bill Roache (Captain). The service of these actors, and of the many tens of thousands of others who have served in the ranks of the Royal Welch Fusiliers, is celebrated and commemorated by the Regimental Museum in Caernarfon Castle.

Lieutenant-General Jonathon Peter Riley,
British Army officer and military historian

rwfmuseum.org.uk
rwfmuseum.org.uk/giving

In the early 1990s, Bill Roache became one of the first celebrities in the UK to recognise that hospice care is a gift—a gift of a comfortable, dignified, and timely passing—a quiet revolution in our thinking about death and dying. And he has used his fame in the best possible way—to raise both awareness and funds—a wonderful legacy that continues to this day.

Nishil Saujani,
Head of Marketing and Communications, Rainbows
Hospice for Children and Young People, Loughborough,
Leicestershire

rainbows.co.uk
rainbows.co.uk/donate

CONTENTS

ACKNOWLEDGEMENTS

The first person we would like to thank is Lieutenant-General Jonathon Riley, Chairman of Trustees, The Royal Welch Fusiliers, and former Colonel of the Regiment, who supported the idea of this book from the beginning, and who substantially contributed to the chapter on Bill Roache's time in their old Regiment. Likewise, we would like to thank the staff of the Royal Welch Fusiliers Museum (Caernarfon, North Wales) for their wonderful assistance, especially Al Poole, Trustee, The Royal Welch Fusiliers Collections Trust, and Karen Murdoch—Collections Manager, Wrexham County Borough Museum and Archive.

A special acknowledgement is extended to Rupert and Nicolas Pullee, proprietors of the Pen y Gwryd Hotel (Snowdonia, North Wales) for hosting the meeting that first inspired our reflection on the times and life of William 'Bill' Roache, and to Nicola Pullee for her extraordinary front cover photographic portrait of Bill Roache.

We would also like to recognise the generous support of the Yogya Santai Cultural Foundation in providing a writer's grant that was fundamental to the success of this project.

To our brilliant publishers, Terrease McComb of The End Publishing Limited (Auckland, Aotearoa New Zealand) and our UK publishing partner Owain Saunders-Jones of Atebol (Wales), we say thank you for your trust in our book and for demonstrating the global reach and continued popularity of *Coronation Street*—from inner-city Salford in the UK to Aotearoa New Zealand in the South Pacific.

In order of their appearance in the book, there are many people to thank for their assistance: Dr Harri Roberts, Tracy Burton, Ni Wayan Murni (Murni's Warung Campuhan-Ubud, Bali), the family of Betty Humphreys (Llanberis, North Wales), Ken Jones, Linus Roache, Verity Roache, Will (James) Roache, Dame Joanna Lumley, Lisa Baker (personal assistant to Dame Joanna Lumley), Michael Fernandez, Shane 'Gonzo' Gonzalez, Martin Winker, Chris Mason, and Dave Ryan (for providing a writers' retreat at the Vanimo Surf Lodge, Sandaun Province (West Sepik) Lido Village, Papua New Guinea, Ben Besant (writer), Professor Joe Moran (Liverpool John Moores University), Bernard and Rosemary Hocking, Craig Glenday and Adam Millward (Guinness World Records), Sarah James (Public Liaison Officer, Rydal Penrhos School), Hannah Patrick (Alumni Liaison and Fundraising Officer, Rydal Penrhos School), Fran Russell (Steiner-Waldorf Schools

Head Office), Matthew Smith (YouGov), Nishil Saujani (Head of Marketing and Communications, Rainbows Hospice for Children and Young People), Dominic Tinner (Relationship Director, Seashell Trust), Jamie Little (Director Variety Golf), Sandra Mattocks (High Profile Support Manager, Brooke, Action for Working Horses and Donkeys), Anthony Lord (Head of Income Generation and Marketing, Willow Wood Hospice), Dame Arabella Warburton, Vanessa Burgess and Liz Meger (Office of Sir John Major), Amanda-Jane Dean (AJ) (Communications and Engagement Manager, ITV in the North), Gerry O'Boyle (The Boogaloo, Highgate), Nikki Heinze (NatCen Social Research UK), Nick Spencer (ComRes Faith Research Centre and Theos Think Tank UK), Brandon Vogt, Aaron Loy, Patrick Collerton (Yipp Films), Ann Rogers (Stride for Truth), Sean Egan (historian and writer), Tracy Strathie (Department for Work and Pensions UK), David Sinclair (Director, International Longevity Centre UK), Caroline Abrahams (Charity Director at Age UK), Kate Winter and Rom Blanco (actors), Frederic James Goodfellow (writer and clinical psychologist), Sinan Bagdatli (writer), Professor John 'Jack' Rowe (Department of Health Policy and Management, Columbia University Mailman School of Public Health), Professor Martin E.P. Seligman (Director, Positive Psychology Center and Zellerbach Family Professor of Psychology, University of Pennsylvania) and Timandra Slade (author and researcher).

Finally, our heartfelt gratitude is extended to Bill Roache, a charming, generous, and humble man without whose close cooperation this book would not have been possible.

FOREWORD

Bill Roache has had strong ties with Wales for most of his life.

At the age of seven, he was enrolled in Rydal boarding school in Colwyn Bay (now Rydal Penrhos—the only Methodist school in the independent school sector in Wales). After 11 years of education, Bill joined a Welsh regiment of the British Army, was commissioned and, after five years of service, reached the rank of Captain.

In 1972, he met our beautiful cousin Sara McEwan Mottram and they found that they had much in common, particularly their mutual links to the mountains of North West Wales. Sara told Bill about her wonderful childhood memories of summers spent with Chris and Jo Briggs (our grandparents) and Brian and Jane Pullee (our parents) in Snowdonia at the Pen y Gwryd Hotel (PyG). Over the years, Bill and Sara enjoyed many happy days together as our family guests. And as you will soon discover, Snowdonia is the sort of spiritual place to which Bill Roache is personally attracted. The name Snowdon is from the Old English for 'snow hill', while the Welsh name *Yr Wyddfa* or 'the tumulus' refers to the stone cairn thrown over the mythical giant *Rhita Gawr* after his defeat by the legendary King Arthur. (For many years Bill had a cottage near Abersoch, a village in the community of Llanengan and a popular seaside resort on the Llŷn Peninsula.)

However, the connection with North Wales extends even further. It was in the PyG's famed Smoke Room that the idea of a fresh approach to biographical writing was first discussed in a meeting between Bill Roache and Dr Rob Goodfellow (who is also our cousin). The result is a 'times and life 90th birthday reflection' that offers readers a balanced historical and social commentary, while also telling intriguing stories about a remarkable individual, punctuated with interesting side facts, references to *Coronation Street*, and humour.

For this reason, we believe that *Reflections on The Times and Life of William 'Bill' Roache* will both entertain and inform and, in doing so, have enduring appeal beyond Bill's fame as an individual.

Rupert and Nicolas Pullee
Proprietors
Pen y Gwryd Hotel, Snowdonia, North Wales
pyg.co.uk

PREFACE

As a team of writers, we have been working on a novel approach to biographical writing for some time. What we call 'reflective times and life' has been well received by readers of our last two books—the first of a famous restaurant in Ubud, Bali and the second of an equally renowned Welsh mountain inn, namely *So Many Delicious Years: Murni's Warung, Ubud, Bali* and *The Pen y Gwryd Hotel: Tales from the Smoke Room.*

For example, the chapter 'Rose, Rose, I Love You' in *So Many Delicious Years* hardly talks about Murni at all (the mother of modern-day tourism on 'The Island of the Gods' and the subject of the book) but rather discusses almost everything around the person of Murni; but Murni is still there and more powerfully portrayed because it is a less is more treatment of the individual. For this reason, *So Many Delicious Years* is as much about the social and cultural context of Murni's life: a changing Bali and a changing world. (The first edition of the book won the prestigious Gourmand Award in 2019.)

Likewise, the chapter 'Girls and Boys and Bicycles' in *Tales from the Smoke Room* tells a heart-warming story about wartime North Wales and the life history of the then 94-year-old Welsh-speaking Betty Humphreys, her story woven around the subject of the legendary 'Home of British Mountaineering'. As with Murni, and the Pen y Gwryd Hotel, our new subject is not necessarily central to the writing. Rather, readers can draw their own conclusions about Bill Roache and the stories we tell. These stories centre on a selection of everyday themes (completely of our choosing) that chart some of the most far-reaching changes in contemporary British society.

The story of Bill's times and life paints a reflective portrait—on topics from soldiering to spirituality and from acting to ageing and one that celebrates the long life of a British television icon while revealing something interesting and insightful about the decades from 9 December 1960 when William 'Bill' Roache first appeared as Kenneth 'Ken' Barlow on that celebrated first episode of *Coronation Street*.

Dr Rob Goodfellow, Jonathan Copeland,
and Peter O'Neill OAM
Wollongong, New South Wales, Ubud, Bali
and Katoomba, The Blue Mountains

William 'Bill' Roache OBE was named in the 2022 New Year's Honours list for 'Services to drama and charity'. (Copyright James Roache, used with permission)

CHAPTER ONE
Zeitgeist

Zeitgeist is a term that means 'spirit of the times'. It can be personified in a dominating individual who characterises any given age. In the history of British television—and certainly in the decades from when the first episode of *Coronation Street* (often referred to as *Corrie*) was broadcast on 9 December 1960—one actor stands out as the epitome of the personified *Zeitgeist* and that is William 'Bill' Roache.[1] Bill's *Coronation Street* character Kenneth 'Ken' Barlow has reflected changes in British society in a way that no other actor or character has, or as Joe Moran, Professor of English and Cultural History at Liverpool John Moores University says, 'Ken Barlow is a fascinating prism through which to read the political and cultural history of the last half century.'

For many people, the character of Ken Barlow has been woven into the fabric of their lives and so has Bill Roache,

---

[1] William Patrick Roache OBE.

who is amongst one of the most recognisable faces in Great Britain—and wherever *Coronation Street* remains popular[2]—acknowledged by *Guinness World Records 2021* (2020) as the 'Longest-serving actor in an on-going drama'.[3]

For some, the fictional Barlow is everything from priggish and humourless, to judgmental and earnest even alienated from his working-class roots by his experience of university—the frustrated, sad-faced, resident academic. For many others, however, the famous character represents something very different. He is reliable Ken, the understanding listener; he is the kind-hearted educated man in the street who cheerfully helps you fill out your passport application; everyone knows someone like that—trustworthy, dependable, and *mostly* sensible, but never boring. Bill Roache is, as his son the actor Linus Roache once said, 'a national treasure'.

Such characters, fictional or real, are more important than we sometimes imagine because while they reflect change they also represent something constant—and, in an uncertain world, constants are rare and reassuring. There

---

[2] *Coronation Street* is shown in Australia (on UKTV), Canada (on CBC Television), Republic of Ireland (on Virgin Media One), Aotearoa New Zealand (on TV One), South Africa (on M-Net City), the US (on Britbox), and through the British Forces Broadcasting Service to British Military personnel and their families serving overseas, which includes the Falkland Islands. *Coronation Street* is also broadcast on the Flemish language TV station Vitaya (Holland).

[3] Craig Glenday and Adam Millward (eds.) *Guinness World Records* (2020), Guinness World Records, London, 2021

is in fact no other character in the contemporary British cultural landscape who can claim such continuity. This is illustrated by the nearly 5,000 episodes of *Coronation Street* that Bill Roache has appeared in as Ken Barlow (as well as featuring in the 1969 *Christmas All Star Comedy Carnival*, in a 1972 US promotion, in the 1985 video *The Jubilee Years*, the 2011 internet episodes of *Ken and Deirdre's Bedtime Stories* and the 2012 charity sketch *Text Santa*).

The *Coronation Street* fictional character Kenneth 'Ken' Barlow was born in 1939 and moved house constantly, the most significant move of which was from the family home at number 3 Coronation Street in 1960 to number 1 in 1972—itself a form of modest symbolic social mobility. (He has also lived in numbers 9, 11, 12, and 15a Coronation Street, in the student halls of Manchester University, in the local pub, in a bed and breakfast, in Glasgow, and somewhere in Canada.)

The son of a postman and a kitchen cleaner, Ken was the original upwardly mobile son of the British working-class. Aspiring to escape his roots, Ken was the first Coronation Street resident to obtain a merit-based grammar school position, and then attend university on a full scholarship. An English and History graduate of The University of Manchester, he began his professional life as a teacher at the fictional Bessie Street School (where he had also been a student). Ken struggled with the teaching profession and took on a variety of jobs, working as a taxi driver, a waiter, a supermarket trolley pusher, a shop assistant, a warehouse manager, a male escort, a Father Christmas, a community development officer, a journalist, and the editor of the local newspaper the *Weatherfield Recorder*—to name but a few of his occupations—foreshadowing real world workforce changes soon to come.

If you look back at that famous first episode, broadcast in humble black and white, you see a snapshot of that year and you sense that the show, and Ken Barlow's journey, will be a harbinger of the tumultuous decade to follow: youth rebellion, the generation gap, the counter-culture movement, and the sexual revolution. But most telling for Ken Barlow and millions of his fellow Britons, was the rapid expansion of a more outward looking, educated, affluent and certainly aspirant, middle-class. Even 'The Street's' theme tune is emblematic. Composed by Eric Spear (for which he was paid £6) the tune was originally called *Lancashire Blues*—itself telling, as Blues music is primarily a call and a response, an action and a reaction, both melancholic and optimistic at the same time.[4] And as Bill Roache has said, 'It really has stood the test of time. The theme somehow works for a funeral, a comedy scene, or a piece of high drama.'

Ironically, the very first newspaper review of the show declared that *Coronation Street* was 'doomed from the outset, with its dreary signature tune and grim scene of a row of Victorian terraced houses and smoking

---

[4] The identity of the trumpeter was not public knowledge until 1994, when jazz musician and journalist Ron Simmonds revealed that it was the Surrey musician Ronnie Hunt.

chimneys'—with the *Daily Mirror's* Ken Irwin going on to claim the series 'would only last three weeks'. But almost everywhere else there was an underlying sense that anything and everything was possible; and that included the fictional community of 'Weatherfield' a town in the northern city of Salford, which is the setting for *Coronation Street*. By the time of the first episode, post-war austerity was at an end and reconstruction was nearing its completion. Things were still bleak in Manchester—or rather Victorian terrace-row inner-city Salford—but there was the expectation and promise of better days ahead—for everyone.

Indeed, Bill notes that *The Observer, The Times,* and *The New Statesmen* referred to 'The Street's' unique synthesis of drama, comedy and social documentary'—a potent, and ultimately enduring formula and a commercial windfall for the newly established Granada Television.

Bill Roache appears as Ken Barlow in that very first episode as a 21-year-old student—eager, handsome, and soon to be fully formed as the archetypical left-liberal, *Guardian*-reading, brown-sauce-rejecting, snooty, junior intellectual. He is at the humble dinner table with his parents. It is a family scene—but the atmosphere is tense. The topic of discussion is class. Frank Barlow (Frank Pemberton) accuses Ken of being embarrassed by his working-class family—in fact, a snob. (Frank is in rolled-up shirtsleeves. Ken is wearing a woollen tie.) Ida Barlow (Elsie Noël Dyson) is working as a cleaner in the Imperial Hotel and Ken plans to take his middle-class girlfriend

Susan Cunningham (Patricia Shakesby) there for a date. Class and generational change are on full display and millions of British households instantly relate. They, in fact, 'got it'.

Frank is angry and confused, Ken is defensive and argumentative; Ida plays the peacemaker; and Ken's younger brother David Barlow (Alan Rothwell) effortlessly represents the meandering sleepy status quo—with his greatest concern in life being a flat bicycle tyre. Ken and 18-year-old Dennis Tanner (Philip Lowrie) from number 11 Coronation Street (who has just been released from six months in prison and can't find a job) head off to the local pub, the incredible Rovers Return Inn, or simply 'the Rovers' to locals, run by the formidable pint puller and local lady Mayoress Annie Walker (Doris Speed), where class continues to prevail as the topic of what is now a very public discussion—generously lubricated by lashings of local ale and fuelled by a seemingly endless supply of delicious pork scratchings.

A fine British balance between conflict and *détente* continues to dominate the episode as Ken Barlow demonstrates his soon to be humanitarian attributes— namely social responsibility in visiting his pensioner friend, the perpetual codger Albert Tatlock (Jack Howarth). The sub-text is that no matter what happens to Ken Barlow, he won't forget 'where 'e came from'. Then all is put right when Elsie Tanner (Pat Phoenix) informs Ken that not only has Susan arrived at the Barlow hearth and home—but that Ken's family 'likes her'. Class war is avoided, and everyone sits down together to a nice cup of tea.

In the less charming real world, as the last of the Baby Boomer generation were being born, the UK had a Conservative Prime Minister Harold Macmillan, and most people were enjoying a relative Age of Affluence where working people 'Never had it so good' (or at least that was what they were told) but there were also the Vassall and Profumo scandals[5] and the threat of nuclear annihilation to keep people occupied—in between *Corrie* episodes. (On 24 January 2022, ITV announced that *Coronation Street* will continue to be broadcast on Monday, Wednesday, and Friday evenings for an hour from 8pm).[6] Young Ken Barlow is preoccupied as well—involved in student street marches and writing a less than appreciated critique of the working-class experience in Weatherfield for the fictitious *Survival Magazine.*

---

[5] William John Christopher Vassall was a British civil servant who spied for the Soviet Union from 1954 until his arrest in 1962. The 'Profumo affair' was a scandal involving John Profumo, the Secretary of State for War in Harold Macmillan's Conservative government, who had an extramarital affair with 19-year-old model Christine Keeler beginning in 1961. Profumo denied the affair in a statement to the House of Commons. A police investigation proved that Profumo had lied. The problem was Keeler was also sleeping with a Russian diplomat, thereby creating a security risk.

[6] Bill says that, 'Far from the quality dropping and 'The Street' drying up, this enriched it; we actually seemed to get a kick, and a rush of adrenaline to the system, when we went to three episodes. The best thing to happen to *Coronation Street* since colour.'

In a literary fit of near-Trotskyite pique, the greenhorn Barlow described his neighbours as 'lazy-minded, politically ignorant, starved of a real culture and prejudiced against any advance in human insight and scientific progress.' (It was a good thing he didn't tell them what he really thought.) Naturally, this didn't go down well and resulted in sly sideways glances, dark looks, and ultimately fisticuffs in the Rovers with the show's original alpha male, beefy builder Len Fairclough (Peter Adamson).

Despite his hyperbole, Barlow had begun to establish his credentials. As Bill says, 'Ken is a liberal, fair-minded guy … who occasionally fights for what he believes is right.' It is curious that commentary on the celebrated fight scene never mentions that the slightly built Barlow gave as good as he got from the heavy-set Fairclough—before the former falls unconscious to the tiles from a knockout blow to the face delivered by the latter.

In the world beyond 'The Street', Prime Minister Harold Macmillan was soon to be followed (after Conservative Prime Minister Sir Alec Douglas-Home) by the steady as she goes, provincial, conservative-socialist Harold Wilson (and a Northerner to boot from Huddersfield, Yorkshire, across the Pennine divide). In some ways, the young Harold Wilson was not unlike the fresh-faced fictional Ken Barlow—the idealistic young teacher from Weatherfield, Lancashire, who likewise captured the admiration and interest of the British public. What was clear, however, was that the cultural centre of gravity in both British politics, and television, had moved from middle-class London to the working-class north, from the sophisticated metropolis to the gritty coal-stained fringe; and Bill Roache was to play a role in practically every major storyline.

His real-life marriage to actress Anna Cropper in 1961, and the birth of their children Vanya and Linus were likewise big news—and so were Bill's many indiscretions. As Bill says, 'There was a great sense of freedom in the air in those days. But with freedom comes responsibility. I had the former but did not exercise the latter.' The show's scriptwriters seized on this and soon Bill Roache was to intrude more into the life of Ken Barlow than Ken Barlow did into the life of Bill Roache.

Not long after, in 1962, fictional Ken Barlow married fictional Valerie Tatlock (Anne Reid). Then in 1964, a very married Ken had a very public flirt with Pip Mistral (Elaine Stevens), a former trapeze artist and exotic dancer at the Kinky Kat Club on Gas Street. It was anarchy; it was anything goes and the British public with their somewhat contemporary ribald sensibilities (think *The Benny Hill Show*) couldn't get enough of it. To paraphrase the American playwright Arthur Miller, *Coronation Street* '… was the nation having a conversation with itself'; and one of the main topics of discussion was—Bill Roache.

In 1965, Valerie Barlow gave birth to twins, Peter and Susan, with Valerie chivalrously driven to the local maternity hospital by none other than good old Len Fairclough—yes, the same Len who gave Ken a good flogging in the Rovers.

Script themes of the day included parenting, women's liberation, and of course male ego—Ken Barlow's ego to be precise. But *Corrie* is a 'soap' after all,[7] or rather, as many (including Bill Roache) prefer to call it, a 'kitchen sink drama', and in November 1965, while Valerie was at a sociology class, no less, Ken is charged with minding the twins.[8] He steps out to the Rovers at the corner of Coronation and Rosamund Streets for a few minutes to buy cigarettes (and no doubt have a pint or two) when a piece of flaming coal falls from the grate, setting fire to the carpet, filling the house with smoke.

Valerie is incensed that Ken had left the babies unattended and says she will leave him if he ever smokes again. For viewers it is cautionary—an indication of change soon to come in the balance of power between the genders, spearheaded as it was on *Coronation Street* by strong female character types as diverse as steely-faced battle-axes Ena Sharples (Violet Carson or Vi to the cast), wise busty barmaids Bet Lynch (Julie Goodyear), and rapid-fire gossiping busybodies such as Hilda Ogden (Jean Alexander). Eventually, Ken and Susan's relationship blew up too and they split shortly after they took part in a 'Ban the Bomb' protest.

---

[7] A soap opera is a radio or television serial that deals with especially domestic themes and is characterised by melodrama. They originated from radio dramas that were sponsored by soap manufacturers.

[8] A 'kitchen sink drama' or 'kitchen sink realism' was a British cultural movement of the late 1950s and early 1960s in film, literature, television and theatre that countered the previously dominant 'escapism' in the performing arts to depict the harsh domestic realities of the working-class.

The flood gates were now open and Ken Barlow immediately set about his business of having numerous 'flings', not to mention a one-night stand with Rita Littlewood (Barbara Knox) and affairs with Jackie Marsh (Pamela Craig), Sylvia Crozier (Avril Angers) and Martha Fraser (Stephanie Beacham), as well as producing a son from his affair with Denise Osbourne (Denise Black) and another child born across the class divide to Susan Cunningham (Patricia Shakesby) which, in grand *Corrie* style, didn't come to light until 2010. Her son, Lawrence Cunningham, was played by Bill's son Linus Roache. Ken's gay grandson James Cunningham was played by Bill's other son James Roache.

Ken Barlow has dated, been engaged, and married so many times that it requires a list to keep track of it all. Such latitude has allowed the writers of *Coronation Street* to explore the many triumphs and tribulations of everyday relationships—including being turned down by Elaine Perkins (none other than the *absolutely fabulous* Dame Joanna Lumley). Generations of scriptwriters have certainly ensured that Ken Barlow's interest in women covered a very wide social spectrum.

Not including those already mentioned, there was a librarian, a secretary, a newspaper reporter, a receptionist, a shop assistant, a student, a graduate, gnarly old Uncle Albert's (Jack Howarth) chiropodist, a café owner, a factory floor unionist, an aspiring actress, a florist, a beautician-stylist, a hairdresser, a single mother, a divorcée, a school headmistress, the chairwoman of the local historical society, and even, as karma would have it, a yoga instructor.

Wendy Nightingale (Susan Tebbs), a married woman from the community centre, also moved in with Ken, making them *Corrie's* first unmarried cohabiting couple. The aggrieved husband, Roger Nightingale (Matthew Long), famously called in to number 11 and punched Ken Barlow on the nose for his trouble. Perhaps Bill Roache, at that time a serial philanderer himself, says it best. 'The trouble is that like any other human being Ken is flawed; we all are.'

In the early 1960s, most of the residents of Coronation Street gathered at the Glad Tidings Mission Hall with the iconic hairnet-wearing, grim-faced resident-sage-caretaker Ena Sharples (Violet Carson) holding centre court. However, by the 1970s, the local place of 'worship' had well and truly moved across the road to the pub of pubs—a perfect alternative universe—a working man's (and woman's) paradise: the Rovers. 'The Street's' characters loved it so much they seemed to be there every day—some all day, and this especially included Ken Barlow. The scene was set for some of British television's most loved and watched storylines that invariably reflected major changes in the very complicated non-fictional world—industrial anarchy, a punishing downturn in the British economy, crippling unemployment, extremist politics, and a rise in domestic and public violence.

In 1970 alone, 'The Street's' scriptwriters covered topics as diverse as secret romances, proposals, engagements, affairs and divorce, an age-gap relationship, murder, suicide, a murder-suicide, a coach crash, debt problems and alcoholism, vandalism, and football hooliganism. However, the real shocker in fictional Weatherfield was a Health Department report that revealed the Rovers was watering down their gin. (And why gin? The locals would have noticed immediately if their delicious pints of Newton and Ridley had been tampered with!)

The 1970s on 'The Street' were like the times—dominated by strong characters, social change, and the complexities of a close-knit community under siege—the ideal canvas for an actor of Bill Roache's calibre. And so, it was to be a busy time for Ken Barlow as well. In April of the first year of that decade, Ken received news that his brother David Barlow (Alan Rothwell) had been killed in a car crash in Australia. One day later, David's son Darren Barlow (only ever seen in on-set photographs) dies too—as a result of the same accident.

The story was highly charged with raw loss and grief, but it also reflected the experience of hundreds of thousands of British people who had, or were about to, emigrate 'Down Under' (many on assisted passages, the so-called 'Ten Pound Poms'[9]) to strange sounding places like Warilla,

---

[9] Following the Second World War, Australia initiated a massive immigration programme, believing that Australia must 'populate or perish'. From the late 1940s, until the early 1970s, hundreds of thousands of displaced Europeans migrated to Australia together with over 1,000,000 British citizens under what was called 'an assisted passage', hence, the 'Ten Pound Poms'. (Some 400,000 people from across the British Isles came to Australia in 1947 alone.)

Wongawilli and Woonona, in search of a better life in the scorching Australian sun. Meanwhile, the cold industrial North of England continued its rapid and heartbreaking decline (beautifully represented in the British blockbuster movies *The Full Monty* and *Brassed Off*).

Here there was a clear nod to a very old theme in British literature—namely the tyranny of distance between Albion and the Antipodes (as represented by Botany Bay convict Abel Magwitch in Charles Dickens's 1861 novel *Great Expectations*). In the autumn of that year, Ken Barlow leaves for New York City to study technical education and, like Abel Magwitch, Ken is out to better himself so that he can ultimately return improved and renewed to assume his role as a community benefactor: Magwitch for Pip, Barlow for the entire street. The very real man, Bill Roache, was soon, however, to embark on his own albeit very different quest for self-improvement, both personal and spiritual. Again, this reflected the *Zeitgeist*—by now the Age of Aquarius—as spirituality and formal religion in Britain, and elsewhere, began to go their separate ways.

But, back on 'The Street', cruel fate in the form of a scriptwriter's typewriter was soon to tragically prevail for Ken and Valerie Barlow. The couple had been planning to move to Jamaica where Ken had been offered a teaching position. (This was yet another nod to the old Empire and to Bill's time as an officer in the British Army when he was stationed there—a deliberate blurring of the lines between actor and character.) But a move to the Caribbean was not to be. Valerie Barlow was unfortunately electrocuted by a nasty combination of a hairdryer, a faulty power outlet, and a knocked over oil heater (for proper dramatic measure). The resulting inferno saw the character literally go up in flames. The next episode ends with Ken making his way through the smouldering remains of their home. It is a memorable scene (deliberately reminiscent of the *Blitz*) and one that Bill Roache describes as amongst his 'most satisfying and dramatic moments on *Coronation Street*'.

The *Zeitgeist* was reinforced yet again as Ken Barlow remarried in 1973. This time to Janet Reid (Judith Barker), in the hope that she would mother his twins. The ambiguity and tension inherent in blended families were clearly in the scriptwriters' minds as the real-world nuclear family was redefined by divorce and remarriage and by common law relationships. (This theme was exemplified 'across the pond' by the American sitcom *The Brady Bunch*, which ran from 1969 until 1974).

In 1974, a failed relationship was reflected in Bill Roache's life too as he and the English stage and television actor Anna Cropper divorced.[10] And it was all very public.

---

[10]Anna Cropper (1938-2007) studied acting at the Central School of Speech and Drama in London. She made her television debut as Chrysalis in *The Insect Play* (1960). She then appeared in *Emergency Ward 10* and on *Coronation Street* in 1962. Cropper came to prominence playing a woman with schizophrenia in the BBC television play *In Two Minutes* (1967) which won the Writers' Guild Award for the Best Television Play of that year. Her film roles included appearances in *All Neat in Black Stockings* (1968), *Cromwell* (1970) and *Nanou* (1986). In 1972, she starred in the television production

The excesses of the 1960s had clearly come home to roost—as it did for many, or even most, of the so-called 'happening generation'. As Bill Roache says, 'I wanted a good, wholesome family life but I misbehaved.' The gossip magazines and the scandal sheet tabloids were full of it, reminding *Coronation Street's* producers, and commercial advertisers alike, of Oscar Wilde's famous quip in *The Picture of Dorian Gray* when Lord Henry says, 'There is only one thing worse in the world than being talked about, and that is not being talked about.' And people continued to talk about Bill Roache—ceaselessly, especially following his successful marriage to actress Sara McEwan Mottram in 1978 and the birth of their three children Verity (born 1981), Edwina (born 1982), and William James (born 1985). Bill was later to write in his autobiography *Ken and Me* (1993) that,

> *Marrying Sara brought about a profound change in me. She transformed me into a man totally satisfied with married life.*

Coronation Street fans took both Bill Roache's shenanigans and his genuine search for redemption as all part of the evolution of the man—and of his alter ego.

---

of *The Exorcism* and, in 1975, took over the lead role in the West End stage version when actress Mary Uren died of an overdose following the play's opening night. She also played Mary Hodgson in the BBC docudrama *The Lost Boys* (1978). Other television roles included two episodes of *Robin Redbreast* (1970), and in *Schmoedipus* (1974). Cropper appeared in *The Jewel in the Crown* (1984) and featured in *Anna of the Five Towers* (1985). Her last television credit was for an episode of *Midsomer Murders* (1999).

And there was no sign of the public growing bored with the character. In 1981, Ken Barlow's wedding to Deirdre Langton (Anne Kirkbride) attracted over 15 million viewers for ITV—more than for the marriage of Prince Charles and Lady Diana Spencer the same year. The timing was a handy coincidence for television ratings. The special *Coronation Street* storyline was a scriptwriters' dream (and a boon for advertisers) as Deirdre was 'British television's sweetheart' while Diana was 'the nation's sweetheart' and the 'People's Princess'. (In contrast, an estimated 14.2 million households watched the royal wedding, about 22.8 million viewers watched Prince William and Kate Middleton's wedding in 2011, and an estimated 29.2 million people tuned in to experience Prince Harry marry the American actress Meghan Markle in 2018.)

Astonishingly, Ken and Deirdre's second marriage in 2005 was watched by over 13 million UK viewers, compared to the 3.6 million who tuned in to Prince Charles' wedding to Camilla Parker Bowles the next day. (Perhaps it was a good thing that the *Coronation Street* producers haven't scheduled Ken Barlow to marry for a fourth time before any other royal weddings.)

The 1980s were to go on to feature some of the most prominent storylines in 'The Street's' history. This included Deirdre Barlow's affair with Ken Barlow's perpetually smug, cockney *bête noire* Mike Baldwin (Johnny Briggs). The storyline attracted intense media commentary, criticism, debate and even professional analysis, especially from marriage guidance counsellors, various pop therapists and even earnest pipe-smoking academic psychologists—an indication of how *Coronation Street* really did function as a reflection of popular culture. And as Bill says, 'As life changes, 'The Street' changes.' The resulting feud between the two men was creative grist for the mill as the character of Ken Barlow continued to develop and mature.

In one famous scene, watched by over 20 million viewers, Bill Roache was given *carte blanche* by scriptwriters to portray his revulsion for the illicit lovers, bad boy Mike Baldwin and loveable Deidre Barlow, an acrimony that was kept alive for an astonishing 19 years. As Ken comes face-to-face with Mike following his discovery of the dalliance, Deirdre dramatically intervenes. Ken attempts to manhandle her. It is a movement of unscripted acting intuition. Ken slams the door shut with his left hand while pushing his wife against the wall with his right, leaving an unprepared Anne Kirkbride visibly shaken, shocked and sobbing.

Bill Roache's performance was ferocious and the cameras just kept rolling. It was unforgettable small screen drama, or as Bill describes it, 'intimate and honest'. And the fans agreed. During a First Division football match, the resolution of the love triangle was put up on Old Trafford's massive electronic scoreboard. The 56,000 strong crowd roared with approval. The scorecard read: 'Ken and Deirdre reunited. Ken 1, Mike 0.'

By 1984, Bill Roache was the last original cast member of *Coronation Street*. A series that had started as 13 episodes, and a six-weeks contract in 1960 extended to six months in early 1961, has continued now for over 60 years. Bill Roache is on record as saying that he only intended to feature in *Coronation Street* for a short time but, once he realised the show's 'colossal impact' he sensed that the drama serial was not only new and different but 'something special'.[11] And indeed, in the minds of legions of *Coronation Street* fans around the world, this sense of the extraordinary has continued across the generations and down to the present day, with groundbreaking storylines such as Ken's relationship with Claudia Colby (Rula Lenska) again foreshadowing a range of *Zeitgeist* possibilities, from Third Age sexuality to challenging the stereotypes that have hitherto defined, or restrained, successful ageing—just two of the many 'times and life' themes that will be explored in this book.

Casting back to 1959, before that famous first episode of *Coronation Street*, BBC producer Olive Shapley and the then 24-year-old scriptwriter Tony Warren were on a train together on their way from London to Manchester when Tony unexpectedly woke her from a nap to say, 'I have a wonderful idea for a television series.' That idea— the story of a working-class terrace house community in

---

[11] An example of this is the groundbreaking *Coronation Street* character Hayley Cropper (Julie Hesmondhalgh) who was the first permanent transgender character in a serialised drama. Her storylines were often meshed with those of the 'Barlow clan'. Her final scenes, which were aired in January 2014, explored the sensitive issue of assisted dying. Hayley Cropper's funeral aired on 31 January 2014. Here we again see the intermingling of Bill Roache's life with fictional characters—his first wife was Anna Cropper.

a cobblestone street somewhere in Greater Manchester incorporating everything from cutting edge drama to light-hearted comedy and social documentary—continues to reflect the spirit of the times, as does the remarkable and enduring acting career of William 'Bill' Roache.

CHAPTER TWO
Genealogy
Secrets and Suprises

The best-known genealogical record can be found in the Bible, although details of the direct descendants of the Chinese philosopher Confucius have been kept up to date for over 2,500 years.[1] The latter is recorded by the *Guinness World Records* as the world's largest family tree, with a staggering 86 recorded generations and over three million direct descendants. The former is recorded in the King James Bible, Matthew 1:2 (in the genealogy of Jesus the Messiah).[2] (However, if you look this one up, be warned, it is a very, very long sentence.)

Genealogy, from the Greek *genealogia* or 'the making of a pedigree', is the study of families, family history and

[1] Confucius (551–479 BCE) is one of the most influential individuals in history. Confucius's teachings and philosophy formed the basis of many East Asian cultures and societies including China, Korea, and Japan.
[2] The Bible records 14 generations in all from Abraham to King David, 14 from King David to the Jewish exile to Babylon, and 14 from the Babylonian exile to the birth of Jesus of Nazareth.

the tracing of their lineages. Since antiquity, genealogy has captured humankind's imagination. Many people, including Bill Roache, have at some time in their lives asked the question, 'Where did I come from?'

A longing to recognise our ancestors seems to be a uniquely human preoccupation. As far as we know, our closest relatives—bonobos, chimpanzees and orangutans—do not concern themselves with this question, although perhaps dolphins and whales do? And so, finding a faded, sepia photograph of two rigid Victorians in the pages of the leather-bound family Bible, on the back of which are written with a fountain pen in neat copperplate, long forgotten names—immediately arouses our curiosity.[3] In the UK, for instance, family history has been described as the second most popular hobby after gardening, and the second major activity on the internet after pornography.

Here we draw a distinction between memory and history. Like many people, Bill Roache can personally recall a swathe of contemporary events defined by happy times as well as by hardship and tragedy. His family home was a large early Victorian house in Ilkeston, a small Derbyshire mining town, which also served as a general practice surgery for two generations of Roache medical doctors.[4] As far as Bill was aware, his ancestors were all 'army, church and medicine'.

---

[3] A style of calligraphic writing.
[4] Ilkeston was founded in the 6th century AD, and is named after its founder, Elka, a local chieftain ('Elka's Tun' or Elka's Town).

Bill was born during the Great Depression[5] when nothing was thrown away and everything was repaired, with everyone, as he says, 'just making do'.[6] Bill's earliest memories are mostly of playing with his older sister Beryl in the family's garden and in their bucolic sunny conservatory. Bill recalls a shady weeping ash, a rope swing, a sand pit, lawns, flowerbeds, a kitchen garden, a greenhouse, garages, and a small rough wooded area.

He especially remembers the commitment and kindness of his general practitioner father to the local community in pre–National Health Service days. This required Bill's father to be on call 24 hours a day seven days a week as well as managing a practice dispensary. (Bill says that all he inherited from two generations of Roache general practitioners was 'hypochondria and bad handwriting'.)

At Rutland House (the Victorian home of Bill's grandparents and parents), there were also hard times with his paternal grandfather and grandmother both dying of Spanish Flu before Bill was born, leaving his father in considerable debt (a reminder of other pandemic days).[7] There was also an

---

[5] The Great Depression started in October 1929 and lasted until the late 1930s (and the outbreak of the Second World War). It was the longest and most socially damaging economic depression of the 20th century.

[6] The lesson of the Great Depression is that if you do not have any debt, if you have some modest savings in the bank (a contingency for unexpected expenses) and if you can live simply, then you will flourish in an economic recession.

[7] The Spanish Flu was an exceptionally deadly global influenza pandemic caused by the H1N1 influenza virus. The first documented illness was in the US in March 1918. Within two years, an estimated

intergenerational history of alcoholism on both sides of his family, especially his paternal uncle. Bill recalls his uncle as 'A dashing extrovert; handsome, good at cricket, football, and swimming, bright at his schoolwork and popular with the girls.' Unfortunately, behind the family's back, Uncle John was living the high life in London and, in the process, he drank his entire medical school tuition allowance.

Bill's own mother had a hard life growing up and her father, Albert, was also a 'heavy drinker' who tragically committed suicide by cutting his own throat. Bill received the terrible news in a letter while at boarding school. He later said, 'I felt sad and cried when I got the news. He had always been there and now he was gone.'

But then, there are the forebears we have never met. Many of us, in fact, wonder about what sort of people our ancestors were. Bill expresses regret that he never met his paternal grandparents, in particular his grandfather who, like his father, was a general practitioner, and much loved by the community.

> *His generosity of spirit was not the only reason I was sad not to have met him. When I began to have an interest in alternative medicines and mysticism, my father (who was also a medical doctor) more than once remarked that I sounded just like my grandfather.*

---

500 million people, or about a third of the world's population, were infected in four waves. The associated death toll was between 17 million to 100 million.

There are many reasons why people search out the histories of their ancestors: to validate family stories, to dispel myths, to find out if they are related to someone famous, to gain a better understanding of an antecedent's involvement in an historical event, to determine genealogical proof of a family connection, to settle questions of inheritance, to trace birth parents, to understand individual health risks or just to better understand themselves—as is the case with Bill Roache.

Interestingly, over time our fascination with ourselves has not diminished. On the contrary, the study of genealogy is increasing as old records are digitised and made available to everyone on the internet. This search requires a knowledge of antiquated laws, old political boundaries, migration trends, and historical, as well as socioeconomic and religious conditions. This can lead in any direction, expanding into an exploration of family myths, ancestors' biographies, lifestyles, and even motivations—and often, as with Bill, uncovering secrets and surprises.

Today, the most diligent genealogists are the Mormons (the Church of Jesus Christ of Latter-Day Saints). They have billions of records that anyone can use to piece together their ancestors' history (familysearch.org). The Mormon site is free and is often the first that professional genealogists turn to.

Everyone has two parents, and each of our parents had two parents, and our four grandparents had two parents each, going back to the beginning of history and into prehistory.

Each generation back, the number of forebears doubles in number.[8] About 10,000 years ago, there lived a man and a woman from whom all Europeans can trace their ancestry. This means that all Europeans are related to Her Majesty Queen Elizabeth II—and even, theoretically, to Jack the Ripper (if he had children) and indeed we are all related to Bill Roache himself. Therefore, the people of the British Isles are a blending of Celt (Cornish, Irish, Manx, Scottish and Welsh peoples), Romans (including the many Middle-Eastern Syrians who made up the bulk of Roman military occupation forces), Angles, Saxons, Jutes, Frisians, Franks, Danes, Goths, Jews, Asians, and Africans and, as the DNA evidence shows, peoples from across the length and breadth of continental Europe. We are in fact all cousins. And close DNA cousins at that.

Intriguingly, the thing is that every person alive today is descended from small communities of geographically dispersed but closely related ancestors. Significantly, the volcanic Toba super eruption, at the site of present-day Lake Toba North Sumatra, Indonesia, which occurred some 75,000 years ago, nearly destroyed our entire species *Homo sapiens*[9] before we could even begin to record our first histories.[10] Evidence suggests that we are

---

[8] It is estimated that in the last 200,000 years there have been between 10,000 and 15,000 generations of *Homo sapiens*. If you include pre-*Homo sapiens* ancestral species, then the number of generations increases over a million years to between 90,000 and 120,000 generations.

[9] Latin for 'wise man'.

[10] Based on the 1998 work of anthropologist Stanley Ambrose, massive environmental changes associated with 'the Toba Event'

all descended from a globally dispersed population of between 1,000 and 10,000 individuals who survived the aftermath of the catastrophe. Indeed, even at the dawn of the first millennium AD, the world's population was only between 150 and 300 million.[11]

It took over 300,000 years for the world's human population to reach one billion, and then only 200 years more to reach nearly eight billion. This means that all human beings can be placed on one family tree. (Scientists can calculate mitochondrial DNA back to one woman who lived about 200,000 years ago from whom everyone is descended and have traced the Y chromosome back to a man we are all related to who lived around 60,000 years ago.)

In their search for pieces of this rich puzzle, the pioneers of modern genealogy, mostly Victorian genealogists, often clergymen on rickety bicycles with too much time on their hands, started with their parents and grandparents, searching birth, death and marriage certificates, baptismal records, court proceedings, children's homes registers, diaries, debtors' roles, hospital admissions and discharges, letters, logs and journals, newspaper reports, prison lists, public obituaries, official census results, parish archives,

---

created significant population bottlenecks with limited genetic variability; this in turn accelerated differentiation of the isolated human populations, eventually leading to the extinction of all the other human species except for the branch that became modern humans.

[11] The largest city in the world at that time was Rome, with a population of around 800,000. And well into the second millennium AD, the global population only grew at a rate of less than 0.1% a year.

ships' manifests, tombstones, war service registers, and anything else they could lay their hands on. Today anyone can draw on this rich trove of historical resources in a few minutes on the internet.

In October 1985, Bill Roache appeared in an episode of *This is Your Life,* the first of the television shows dedicated to genealogy and life histories.[12] The iconic Irish host, Eamonn Andrews, with his famous 'big red book' in hand, surprised Bill dressed as an Arab sheik accompanied by an actual camel during a cast photo shoot to celebrate *Coronation Street's* 25th anniversary—an obvious reference to Bill's army days.[13]

More recently, internationally syndicated television programmes, such as *Who Do You Think You Are?*, have reflected this continuing curiosity and illustrate that we are not only fascinated in ourselves and our own ancestors but, like *This is Your Life*, also by the family trees and intimate lives of others. (An interest in the lives of celebrities also exposes a bit of harmless genetic voyeurism.)

---

[12] The internationally syndicated show, based on the 1952 American production of the same name, which ran with Eamonn Andrews as UK host from 1955 until 1964 and again from 1969 until his death in 1987. Michael Aspel then took up the role of host until the show ended in 2003. It briefly returned in 2007 as a one-off special presented by Trevor McDonald. In all there were 1,130 episodes.

[13] There is an interesting backstory to the episode. The 'red book' was misplaced and Eamonn Andrews was forced to quickly adapt in the minutes before filming began by holding a substitute black leather ledger that was at hand.

Who Do You Think You Are?, featuring Bill Roache, was broadcast on 26 September 2012. The show revealed much of what was already known and written about Bill, including that his great-grandfather, Joseph Matthew Roache, was born in 1842 in Cashel, Tipperary, Ireland. He was a Lieutenant in the British Army named on an Ordnance Store Department document dated 1885 (and later in a British Army list of 1900 as a Captain—as later was Bill's rank too).

Interestingly, on the 1891 census, Bill's maternal great-grandfather James Waddicor is described as both a 'phrenologist'[14] and a 'medical electrician'[15] who practised his 'profession' in Blackpool. At the time, it was believed that electricity could cure many ailments. Before that, he is listed in the 1881 census as a quarryman and grocer in Darwen, Lancashire. James Waddicor seems to have reinvented himself as an entrepreneur, leaving an estate to his wife and daughter-in-law—but significantly, not to his son Albert.

---

[14] In the 19th century, phrenology was promoted by George Combe (1788–1858), who had worked briefly as a lawyer and a brewer in both the UK and the US as a means of determining a person's basic characteristics, especially by examining the shape and cubic volume of his skull. The idea was fashionable for a couple of decades but is now completely discredited.

[15] The first recorded treatment of a patient by electricity was in 1743. For a time, electrical treatment was promoted as a universal panacea but was rejected by mainstream medicine except for use in the treatment of 'insanity'. Today electroconvulsive therapy (ECT) is mostly used in patients with severe major depression or bipolar disorder.

The highlight of the programme were surprising revelations about Bill's grandmother, whom he describes as 'a towering personality' and 'the power in the family'. Bill knew that she ran a café but not that she was a 'trailblazing entrepreneur'. Unfortunately, Albert Waddicor (Bill's maternal grandfather) was not just 'a heavy drinker' but a violent alcoholic. His occupation is listed in the 1911 census as, rather ironically, 'selling ices and temperance (non-alcoholic) drinks', together with his wife from a 'shanty shop' on Blackpool's Golden Mile. Bill says that Albert was so bad that, at just three months of age, Bill's mother Hester was sent to live with an aunt in Leigh, Staffordshire, for protection from him.

Despite this, Bill's grandmother went on to become a highly successful businesswoman running tea rooms in the Alton Towers mansion in the 1920s and 1930s, long before it became a landmark theme park. At one time, in fact, Zillah's restaurant offered dining for more than 1,000 people at a single sitting with over a quarter of a million visitors annually.[16] (Because of demand, the local railway station had to be enlarged.) As Bill says,

> *I loved all that I discovered about my grandmother Zillah and was surprised how important and successful she was. She was one of the first British female entrepreneurs and one of the first to open stately homes to the public. I would stay at Alton Towers with my parents when it was not open, and I*

---

[16] Zillah became the licensee in 1925, and in 1933 she also took on the Old Mill Buffet in Alton.

would have the run of the place. In her old age, Zillah came to live with us but died shortly afterwards. To me she was just a lovely old granny who would take me to buy an ice cream. In the future, I hope to trace my ancestry further back, especially on my father's side with the succession of doctors and vicars and the connection to Rudolph Steiner.

However, the story of Bill Roache's genealogy doesn't end there. Thanks to the publication of the first complete human genome in 2001 (which took hundreds of scientists almost ten years to complete at a cost of over US$3 billion) we can now get a more complete picture of just who Bill Roache is by also looking at his DNA—or rather his 'genetic history'.

Today, for less than US$100 you can spit into a small plastic tube and have your genome sequenced, including your Neanderthal DNA. (That's because *Homo sapiens* interbred with the Neanderthals.) Not only is Neanderthal DNA found in us, but *Homo sapiens* DNA[17] is found in millennia-dead Neanderthals.[18]

One notable case that attracted global interest in DNA testing was that of English King Richard III. The bones of Richard, the last of the Plantagenet monarchs, were

---

[17] The structure of DNA was discovered in 1953 by James Watson and Francis Crick; however, the molecule now known as DNA was first identified in the 1860s by the Swiss chemist Johann Friedrich Miescher.

[18] For most Europeans, the average amount of Neanderthal DNA is 2.7%.

identified using this same technology. Richard was born in 1452 and killed in 1485 by Henry Tudor's men at the Battle of Bosworth Field[19] during the 32-year-long Wars of the Roses (May 1455 to June 1487). In 2012, his remains were found in a Leicester Social Services' car park covering the site of the former Greyfriars Church and were identified based on a DNA sample from two distant maternal descendants, as well as corroboration with other archaeological, historical and scientific evidence.[20]

Today, tens of millions of people around the world have also had their DNA analysed including the cast of *Coronation Street*. The 90-minute television special *Coronation Street's DNA Secrets* was presented by Nicky Campbell and broadcast on 5 September 2018 on ITV. The cast were invited to explore their ancestral background by giving a saliva sample. They were then presented with their DNA results at three iconic *Coronation Street* sets—the Rovers, Roy's Rolls and Nick's Bistro.[21] The show also united the cast with fans who happened to be distant relatives. (Bill was introduced to a distant Irish cousin.)

Bill's DNA profile showed the following: Great Britain 37%, Scandinavia 28%, Western Europe 18%, Ireland, Scotland and Wales 15%, the Iberian Peninsula and Finland both 1%. While intriguing, genealogists say that such raw genetic data is only a part of one's pedigree—

---

[19] Near Ambion Hill, south of Market Bosworth, Leicestershire, England.
[20] Richard is now buried in Leicester Cathedral.
[21] Now 'The Viaduct Bistro.'

best understood by incorporating and corroborating more recognised forms of historical evidence. However, DNA testing is now clearly a large piece of the puzzle of better understanding who we are.

According to Bill's DNA report, the average Briton's genetic make-up is 36.6% Anglo-Saxon/Great Britain, with most of the remaining DNA coming from Europe and Ireland. Interestingly, Yorkshire is genetically the 'least European' part of England, with 57.98% of its DNA originating from Europe while Scotland stands out as the 'most European' region of the British Isles, with the average Scottish resident's European DNA being as high as 71.89%.[22]

While Bill Roache's DNA profile may be 'typical' of today's English people—the story of his near forebears, including the remarkable Mary Zillah Waddicor, is anything but, and this is an intriguing indication of what other surprises may be in store should Bill, or his children, continue to ask the question, 'Where did we come from?'

---

[22] This raises the immediate question: is this one of the reasons why Scotland voted to remain with Europe?

CHAPTER THREE
Education
Three Cheers for Aesthetics

For an actor, timing is everything. In managing to be born in 1932, Bill Roache found himself in perhaps one of the best times for a middle-class child in England to be both educated and informed. In that year, the Roache family, like many at home and abroad, began to consider the 'wireless' as their main source of news, views, and entertainment.

To put the world of his early years into perspective, the British Empire covered over 35 million square kilometres with colonies on every continent, not including Antarctica.[1] This can be compared to the Roman Empire's five million square kilometres, which stretched from the Nile to Britannia at its maximum expanse under Emperor Trajan, who reigned from 98 to 117 AD.

---

[1] The UK's formal claim on Antarctica dates to 1908 and the Falkland Islands Dependencies Letters Patent 1843, which remains the oldest formal territorial claim on the Antarctic continent.

To meet the necessities of a colonial power that coloured a quarter of the world map pink (because red made it difficult to read place names like Kanahooka, Koonawarra and Katoomba), in mid-December 1932, the BBC Empire Service, later known as the BBC World Service, began utilising the shortwave radio facility at Borough Hill, Daventry, Northamptonshire, to reach a global English-speaking audience of enthusiastic listeners in places like Wagga Wagga, Wandandian and Wollongong. Two weeks later, on Christmas Day, His Majesty King George V delivered the very first royal Christmas message on the Empire Service live from Sandringham House (written by the Nobel Prize Laureate, Rudyard Kipling of *Captain Courageous, Gunga Din* and *The Jungle Book* fame). The broadcast was heard by over 20 million subjects across the Empire in places like Newfoundland, New South Wales, and Aotearoa New Zealand. (Radio was effectively the internet of the age.)

To this day, the Christmas message remains one of the few occasions when the sovereign speaks publicly without advice from a minister of the Crown. That's because it is her personal message as head of the Commonwealth. (The Queen's 2020 Christmas message—which focused on hope amid the pandemic, topped the UK TV ratings with over eight million viewers. However, on BBC One, ITV and Sky News, *Coronation Street* attracted a very respectable 4.55 million viewers, well ahead of rivals *Emmerdale* and *EastEnders*.)

*****

Bill was seven years old when the Second World War broke out. He remembers gathering around the radio in the sitting room with his family listening to the declaration of War with Germany.[2] He also revealed that his father would tune into the then BBC Home Service and move small, coloured flag pins to chart the progress of British forces on a wall map at their Rutland House home.

At the age of four in 1936, as war seemed increasingly likely in Europe, young Bill started kindergarten in the newly established progressive Michael House Steiner-Waldorf School, built on land donated by his grandfather. (His 'pioneering grandfather' was interested in 'all things spiritual' as were Bill's great aunts Mable and Mickey.) Michael House, while strictly a private school, was co-educational, open to all, independent and as far as it was possible, free from government interference.[3] It was part of an Austro-German-inspired worldwide movement, but

---

[2] The UK declared war on Germany on 3 September 1939, two days after the German invasion of Poland. The state of war was announced to the British public through a radio broadcast delivered by the prime minister Neville Chamberlain. The text was as follows: 'This morning the British ambassador in Berlin handed the German government a final note stating that unless we heard from them by 11 o'clock that they were prepared at once to withdraw their troops from Poland, a state of war would exist between us. I have to tell you now that no such undertaking has been received, and that consequently this country is at war with Germany.'

[3] The first Waldorf school opened in 1919 in Stuttgart, Germany. Since this time, it has become the largest independent school movement in the world, with more than 1,200 independent schools and nearly 2,000 kindergartens located in 75 countries, as well as more than 500 centres for special education in more than 40 countries.

as Steiner education was individualistic, internationally oriented, and pacifist, the Nazis closed all their schools in Germany after the *Anschluss* in 1938 and the remainder across Axis-occupied Europe after 1940.[4]

In another chapter, we will discuss the influence of Michael House on the later development of Bill Roache's spirituality, however, in describing his broad experience of Steiner education, we can do no better than to use Bill's own words.

> *Rudolf Steiner schools worked towards developing harmonised individuals, with music and art regarded as of greater value than academic facts. There were no punishments that I remember, but responsibility for your own actions and caring for others were impressed from the beginning. Nor was there any overt religious teaching but a strong spiritual air permeated everything we did. The place was full of music, light, colour, and kindness.*

Bill Roache entered school at a time of increasing concern about education in Britain. Sir Henry Hadow, who was Vice-Chancellor of the University of Durham from 1916 to 1918, and the University of Sheffield from 1919 to 1930, was commissioned by the government to produce six reports between 1923 and 1933, which contained

---

[4] Hitler's own disdaining remarks regarding Rudolf Steiner appeared as early as 1921. In 1933, Steiner's books were banned from public libraries in Bavaria and then later publicly burned elsewhere in Germany.

1,500 pages of mostly progressive submissions, notably *The Education of the Adolescent* (1926) and *The Primary School* (1931).

What became known as the *Hadow Committee Reports* made recommendations concerning the provision and availability of books and playing fields, the design of buildings and classroom sizes, the introduction of intelligence tests (since discredited), as well as the accreditation of professional teaching qualifications. The reports also recommended a break between junior and elementary school at age 11 and the introduction of free secondary education.

Not surprisingly for the times, Hadow considered that there should be different requirements for boys and girls. (Girls were to be protected from 'physical fatigue' and 'nervous overstrain' so that they could concentrate on domestic duties.) However, in terms of Bill's interest in school theatre or the later possibility of him even thinking about acting as a serious career, one of Hadow's recommendations was to be life-changing.

Hadow argued that the standard curriculum was too academic and proposed that more attention should be given to 'aesthetics,' and that this needed to involve students pursuing their own interests. This really was progressive thinking. (Significantly, from 1927 to 1930, the number of pupils in England aged between eight and 12 increased from 150,000 to 400,000, that is from 7% to 16% of the total child population.)

Bill Roache was indeed one of the fortunate ones. In 1934, only 119 in a thousand elementary pupils in England had a secondary school place at age 11. In that year, there were 448,421 pupils in secondary schools. Of these, 216,255 had free places, 15,152 had a partial remission of fees, and 217,014 had parents who paid their fees in full. From the middle of the 19th century, the ruling-classes in Britain had doggedly resisted universal education. Rather, they preferred to indenture juveniles from the lower classes in their factories and mines. Children were cheap labour. Despite resistance from industrialists, in 1922 the school leaving age in the UK was raised to 14 but was not increased to 15 until 1947. (Perhaps under pressure to garner even greater profits from their 'dark satanic mills' the captains of industry were experiencing their own nervous overstrain.)[5]

In 1939, at the age of seven, Bill followed his cousin, Harry Nicholson,[6] and became a junior (preparatory) boarder at Beech House, part of the independent Methodist Rydal School (later the co-educational Rydal Penrhos School) in Colwyn Bay, North Wales. (Harry's sister Audrey was already a border at Penrhos.) It was wartime and over a million children were evacuated from the big cities of Britain— mostly London, Liverpool, Manchester, Birmingham, Leeds, and Sheffield—and so were mostly children from

---

[5] William Blake, 'and did those feet in ancient time', from the preface to his epic *Milton: A Poem in Two Books* (1808).

[6] Harry Nicholson's parents ran the Northwick Arms Hotel in Evesham where, as children, Bill and his sister Beryl used to stay for a week every year. Bill says, 'He was quite a character and was the official rat catcher when Rydal was evacuated to Oakwood Park during the War.'

the urban working-class. They were despairingly referred to as 'vacees' (evacuees) by the upper-class Rydal boys but, by all accounts, gave as good as they got.

Bill was able to stay on at Rydal, (although moved for safety to the Oakwood Park campus) but like all children in the UK at the time, regardless of social class, he had regular gas-mask drills. (The government produced a specially designed brightly coloured version for children that sort of looked like Mickey Mouse. It must have been terrifying.) He also learnt to throw himself under his flimsy wooden desk in case of a direct hit by a 250 kg *Sprengbombe Cylindrisch* in a Luftwaffe air raid;[7] and like everyone else in Britain, he experienced food rationing.[8] (In a later parallel to the Barlow back story, his fictional mother Ida Barlow [Elise Noël Dyson] gave birth to him, on 9 October 1939, unaided, under the kitchen table during an air raid drill.)

Rydal was a boys only school. (Penrhos was the equivalent girls' school where Bill Roache's older sister Beryl was a student.) By all accounts, he was a diligent pupil and received a good grounding in the core subjects that, thanks to Hadow, now included art, music, English, and French. In his second autobiography, *Soul on the Street*, Bill fondly recalls one of his favourite teachers, Ms Olive James, a war widow, who tutored him from her own home in Llandudno in his least favourite subject of biology (after his next least favourite subjects of chemistry and

---

[7] On 23 May 2019, a live SC250 was discovered during construction works near Kingston University Campus, London.

[8] Rationing did not formally end in the UK until 1954.

physics). This was in anticipation of him following his 'august predecessors' into St. Bartholomew's Hospital Medical College. However, as it turned out, Bill was less than enthusiastic about the prospect of becoming a doctor and Rydal was happy to nurture his other more aesthetic interests. As he says,

> It would be good to say there had been a strong vocational calling to do drama. There hadn't, not at that point. But I know that nothing happens by accident and that there is no such thing as a coincidence.

The Rydal School Centenary Register includes a reference to ROACHE, William Patrick (actor), noting that he was a prefect, head of house, and played cricket and rugby for the school. He was a right-handed opening batsman but was a slow left-handed bowler and played scrum-half and wing-forward in rugby. Significantly for his later career in the performing arts, he studied music and won the school drama prize. Years later, Bill Roache as Ken Barlow, played the trumpet for over 16 million viewers, first at a *Coronation Street* Christmas concert in Ena Sharples' (Violet Carson) mission hall and later when the character Ernie Bishop (Stephen Hancock) formed a band and invited him to join. The tune was *Yellow Bird*, which Bill later self-deprecatingly said he 'murdered'.

A survey of annual dramatic productions at Rydal during the years that Bill was a senior student at Oakwood Park campus (1946-1951) presents an interesting reflection of contemporary British theatrical sensibilities. It includes *She Stoops to Conquer* (a comedy by Oliver Goldsmith first performed in 1773), *Julius Caesar* (William Shakespeare), *The Winslow Boy* (a drama based on a true story by Terence Rattigan about family honour), *Murder in the Cathedral* (adapted from the book of the same name by T. S. Eliot about the assassination of Thomas Becket), *Macbeth* (William Shakespeare) ('the Scottish play' to Bill Roache),[9] *The Headmaster* (a popular farce by Edward Knoblock and Wilfred Coleby) and finally, *You Never Can Tell* (a four act comedy by George Bernard Shaw).

Interestingly, Bill Roache's views on superstition and the Scottish play are that,

---

[9] Actors are a superstitious lot. *Macbeth* has always been considered 'unlucky'. It's where the safe world of the stage (where actors breathe life into characters) transforms itself and endangers the players. Many actors believe that witches, annoyed that Shakespeare used real spells in several scenes, cursing the play itself. Many will not utter the play's title and rather call it 'The Scottish play' nor do they say the names of any of its characters. They call Macbeth 'The Thane' and Lady Macbeth 'The Queen'. Many actors won't wear costumes that have been worn on stage in a previous production. Accidents have happened since the play was first performed around 1606. Indeed, at the very first production Lady Macbeth died and Shakespeare himself had to play the role. Real murders have been committed, such as when a real dagger was used to kill Duncan, instead of a theatrical prop. Fires have broken out. Scenery has fallen, as happened to Laurence Olivier in 1937 at the Old Vic. An actress playing Lady Macbeth decided to play the sleepwalking scene with her eyes closed to make it more realistic. She walked straight off the edge of the stage and crashed into the orchestra pit, seriously hurting herself. Fortunately, you can reverse catastrophe if you utter the name of the play by mistake. Leave the theatre, spin around three times, spit, curse and then knock on the theatre door to be allowed back in.

Many people do not understand of the power of thought. If a strong belief is held, the energy of that belief will attract itself to the believer. If you don't believe it, then normal circumstances prevail. It takes a very positive, entrenched belief to be effective. The Scottish play is no exception. I am aware of its presence but have no experience of its effects.

*****

Rydal was a public school, that is to say, a private school, which, like all public schools, benefited from a range of generous endowments. Today this contrasts with state-funded comprehensive schools, and a slowly dwindling number of state-funded academically oriented selective grammar schools. And, although their pupils were mostly drawn from wealthy families, public schools enjoyed charitable status, which in turn qualified them for indirect grants of public money as well as immense tax advantages. Yet they remained largely outside state control and supervision—and, in the case of Rydal, proudly so. Methodists were, after all, amongst the original 'non-conformists'. Rydal boasted an eclectic but impressive group of alumni and, like other public schools, offered part scholarships for a small number of less affluent children—often as not middle-class children with sporting or musical talent, rather than bright children of the working-class (not unlike the character of Ken Barlow).

Far from Britain's public schools, in gritty working-class *Coronation Street*, a chasm clearly existed at the time between the different opportunities available to

Bill Roache and Ken Barlow. Ken attended Bessie Street Comprehensive School, (formally Silk Street Elementary and Hardcastle's Factory School), went on to grammar school after passing his eleven plus exam, and then won a merit-based scholarship to the University of Manchester, where he graduated with a second-class honours degree in English and History, becoming the first resident of his fictitious community to gain a tertiary qualification. (In the real world, the University of Manchester is a very prestigious public [not private] institution, boasting some 25 Nobel Laureates amongst its past and present students and teaching staff, with some of the most important discoveries of the modern age having been made there, particularly in physics and chemistry).

In many ways, the fictional young Ken Barlow represents the antithesis of the English public school experience—which must have been in the Granada Television writers' minds as they devised the nuts and bolts of the famous character and distinctions and similarities between Bill and Ken began to take form. In one *Coronation Street* episode in 2008, Ken Barlow's adult son, Peter Barlow (Chris Gascoyne), turns up drunk to his own child's Bessie Street School nativity play and causes havoc, which is not something you can imagine happening at a Rydal Methodist School parent-teacher night.[10]

*****

---

[10] Peter Barlow has been played by a total of seven actors, John Heannau (1965–1970), Christopher Dormer (1970–1971), Mark Duncan (1971), Linus Roache (1973–1975), Joseph McKenna (1977–1978), David Lonsdale in 1986 and Chris Gascoyne (2000–the present).

What distinguished Rydal from similar institutions was that, from its foundation in 1880, it was characterised by self-disciplined, benevolent and evangelical Methodism. Still, some practices that now horrify contemporary society were once commonplace across the entire public school system. For example, Bill recalls one of his teachers' efforts to 'rectify' his left-handedness.[11]

> *My teacher Miss Corbett ordered me to use my right hand only, and if I was caught writing left-handed, it was rapped with a wooden ruler. This had quite a bad effect on me. Apart from delaying my ability to write properly by a year or so, the tension brought on a temporary stammer. (Apparently, King George VI had a stammer caused the same way. The same treatment didn't work for him either and the King's stammer remained). I was greatly relieved after moving out of Miss Corbett's class to be allowed to revert to my natural left-handedness.*

Soon afterwards, Bill's stutter and his dyslexia completely resolved.

Bill also comments that corporal punishment (caning) was initially part of Rydal school life until a new

---

[11] Until recently, 'left'—or the left side—was widely considered the lesser aspect and so was associated with darkness, demons, and evil. The Latin word 'sinister' in fact means 'on the left side'. Alternately, the Latin word 'dexter,' means 'on the right side' and carries a positive connotation, as with the popular expressions, 'the right thing to do', and 'the right side of history'.

headmaster named Donald Hughes had it banned.[12] Bill Roache was clearly influenced by the practical Christianity of the longtime headmaster who, by all accounts, exemplified the Rydal motto *prodesse quam conspici* or, 'to accomplish rather than be conspicuous'. He later described his headmaster as 'sensitive by nature and liberal by inclination' and 'the epitome of fairness and kindness'. Percy Heywood's biography of Donald Hughes (1970) notes that, 'No boy passed through the school in his time without being confronted with the virtues of humble and unselfish service to God and man'—although it must be said there was friction between the two.[13] Bill was clearly not willing, even as a child, to accept religious dogma without question.

> *I couldn't help myself but to challenge the theology master—I was possibly the most irritating pupil he had, always wanting answers.*

It is important to say that, on balance, Bill Roache's experience of public school was a positive one. (Indeed, so positive that he enrolled his eldest son Linus at Rydal between 1980 and 1982.) There were however omissions, again consistent with the times. In those days, no formal sex education or instruction was provided at Rydal. Bill instead had to rely on other boys to explain

---

[12] Corporal punishment was not abolished in state schools in England until 1986 and not until 1999 in all independent schools.
[13] Percy Heywood, (1970) *Donald Hughes Headmaster: Selected Writings with a Personal Portrait*, Rydal Press, Colwyn Bay.

'the mechanics.'[14] And the archaic custom at Rydal of communal cold summer baths for junior boys was just plain weird—supervised as they were by the school matron herself. (At least this seems strange to us today.) The stated purpose was 'character building'.

Unfortunately for Bill, the possible psychological harm caused by his teacher's misguided efforts in forcing him to use his non-dominant right hand may have inadvertently contributed to his bed wetting. There were four bedwetters in his junior class and they were all put together in the same dormitory to minimise embarrassment (presumably to them). In *Ken and Me,* Bill writes, 'Only another sufferer can know the ignominy, embarrassment and helplessness of such an affliction,' but 'knowing that there were fellow sufferers was a comfort.' Again, this appears to be a testimony to Donald Hughes's compassionate influence on boys like Bill.

It is interesting to compare Bill's experience of public school with that of George Orwell, written about his earlier years just before and during the First World War.[15] Chronicled in his essay, 'Such, Such Were the Joys' (first published in 1952), Orwell paints a dismal picture of public school life that, he forcefully wrote, was defined by

---

[14] The first sex education course at a British school started in 1889 at Abbotsholme, a progressive public school in Rocester, Derbyshire, however, sex education did not become mainstream until well after the Second World War.

[15] George Orwell won a scholarship to England's foremost public school Eton, founded in 1440 by King Henry VI, and became a King's Scholar from 1917 to 1921.

cruelty and snobbery and cold baths, as well as beatings with a riding crop for bedwetting—overall a soul-destroying experience.[16] In contrast, Bill says that life at Rydal, 'actually strengthened my character.'

*****

The historical corollary to Bill's experience of public school is that, while such institutions were originally endowed and established to provide an education for the poor, public schools in England began to see their role primarily as educating, and even creating, the ruling-classes. They came into their own between the 1870s and the 1930s during the zenith of the British Empire, churning out boys schooled in the classics, and not much else, but with stiff upper lips and the necessary athletic stamina to exercise a 'God-given right' to rule the world. (In Scotland, there was a tradition of the gentry sharing their primary education with tenants, which made for a more egalitarian system.)

The famous epigram attributed to the Duke of Wellington, 'The battle of Waterloo was won on the playing fields of Eton', was probably apocryphal, however the message was clear—the future ruling-classes were best 'nurtured' in a public school environment and, in turn, the 'old boy network' could be relied on to defend the nation and the interests of the ruling-classes, which were considered by them to be one and the same. (This however was not

---

[16] George Orwell, *Selected Essays*, Oxford University Press, Oxford, 2021.

completely true, rather it is the 'cannon fodder'—or the 'PBI' [the poor bloody infantry] who fight and win wars).

A question this raises is, are great characters born or made? Or both? As one of the first writers to discuss the idea of 'nature versus nurture' in fiction, D.H. Lawrence put words into the mouth of the aristocratic Sir Clifford in *Lady Chatterley's Lover*, originally published in 1928, which emphasise that, in Sir Clifford's opinion, the child's environment is much more important than the child's parentage. Sir Clifford could not have children and was contemplating the possibility of his wife Connie becoming pregnant by another man and giving birth to a child, hopefully a son, who could inherit, be accepted by him, and continue the aristocratic Chatterley line. The dialogue is revealing and worth investigation.

It is not who begets us that matters, but where fate places us. Place any child among the ruling-classes, and he will grow up, to his own extent, a ruler. Put kings' and dukes' children among the masses, and they'll be little plebeians, mass products. It is the overwhelming pressure of environment.

Bill Roache, like generations of other privileged children, must have often looked up at the stained-glass memorial window in the Rydal dining hall that recorded the names of 63 such 'nurtured' individuals—'Old Rydalins'—all young men of the upper-classes, and almost all junior army officers who sacrificed their lives for King and Country in the First World War. (The school memorial for the Second World War contains 43 names, most of whom were RAF pilots or bomber crew.)

The reality was that public schools perpetuated, and even refined, class divisions in English society—as is still very much the case today. Public schools are expensive, and largely insulated from wider society by what is effectively an educational and financial apartheid. For example, in 2018–2019, the basic yearly fees for Eton were £40,668, Harrow £40,050 and Winchester (founded in 1382) £39,912, well above the average annual salaries of most Britons.

In 1944, during Bill Roache's school days, only 2% of the country's population attended a public school, while 56% of all Members of the House of Commons at the time were public school boys. Most of the population, including almost all women and girls, had only the most basic education: 92% attending elementary school only. This was reflected in the fact that women contributed a mere 3% of candidates who stood at a General Election before 1945.[17]

The Second World War engendered widespread criticism of the public school system that continues to the present day. The institutions were supposed to create well-rounded leaders, but the reality was often very different. Rather, they gave their high fee-paying pupils effortless self-confidence,

---

[17] Viscountess Astor, the American-born British politician Nancy Witcher Langhorne Astor, was not the first woman elected to the Westminster Parliament (1919). Rather it was Countess Constance Markievicz (born Constance Georgine Gore-Booth) who was elected in 1918, but as she was an Irish Republican, a member of Sinn Fein, and an inmate of Holloway Prison at the time, she 'declined' to take her seat.

feelings of superiority and seamless privilege, often without merit. Even Winston Churchill, an aristocrat himself, and an Old Harrovian, recognised the need for reform. And so, although the country was at war, engaged in a life and death struggle with Nazi Germany, his government passed the momentous, comprehensive landmark Education Act 1944 that replaced almost all previous relevant legislation and set the framework for post-war education in England and Wales. Most importantly, it established a nationwide system of free (comprehensive), compulsory schooling for children between the ages of five and 15. And it provided that the leaving age should be raised to 16 'as soon as practicable', although this did not happen until 1973— because clearly it was not so practicable.

Despite the universal availability of a state-funded basic education in England, even today public school influence remains plainly evident. For example, former British Prime Minister David Cameron (in office 2010-2016), was a born Etonian. (The fact he went to Eton is probably the single most notable thing people remember about him.) His father was at the school before him, and his grandfather before him and on his mother's side his grandfather, great-grandfather, great-great-grandfather and even his great-great-great-grandfather. (David Cameron was not so much 'born with a silver spoon in his mouth' but, it seems, an entire cutlery service.)[18]

---

[18] The original quote is attributed to former Australian Prime Minister Paul Keating (1991-1996) who once described the then leader of the Conservative Opposition Alexander Downer as, 'The idiot son of the Adelaide aristocracy, born not with a silver spoon, but an entire cutlery service in his mouth.'

The Education Act was an astounding achievement and gave hope to millions of working-class children and, in turn, became a cornerstone of the Welfare State. The Labour Party, led by Clement Attlee, a public school boy himself (Haileybury) and an Oxford graduate, had won the 1945 General Election by a 10.7% landslide (shocking the born-to-rule conservatives under Winston Churchill). Ironically, Clement Attlee was then responsible for implementing the already legislated reforms, and so got the credit. And even though it meant more teachers and greater, expensive infrastructure, there were no objections from the Tories.

The Act also significantly provided free school meals and fresh milk, as well as medical and dental treatment. It did not, however, contain anything of any significance about public schools, which were left mostly intact and undisturbed. For the elite public service decision makers in Whitehall, all of whom, probably without exception, were public school boys and graduates of Oxford or 'the other place,' (Cambridge) it really was a case of, to quote an Americanism, 'If it ain't broke, don't fix it.' (Think of the characters Sir Humphrey Appleby and Bernard Woolley of *Yes Minister* fame.) In fact, the increasing affluence of the middle-class after the Second World War resulted in even greater numbers of public school pupils, Bill Roache and his son Linus Roache amongst them.

So, has anything changed since Bill Roache's school days? According to Professor David Kynaston and Professor Francis Green in their book *Engines of Privilege, Britain's*

Private School Problem (2019),[19] today only 7% of the UK's total school population attends a public school, however, one in seven teachers works in a public school and one pound in every six of all school expenditures in England directly benefits public schools. (As an extreme example, they cite the Sutton Trust publication *Leading People* (2016) that reports 74% of UK judges are privately educated— which might be a bad illustration as it takes years to even be considered as a judge and so most of today's judges are more representative of education in the 1990s and possibly do not represent the current state of play.)[20]

With the jobs boom of the late 1980s, and subsequent skills shortages, profit-driven employers will hire just anyone they can get. And, as novel as it sounds, (like today) they really did want the 'best person for the job' regardless of whether the candidate was educated at public school or not.[21] The days of jobs for the boys seemed to be over.[22] The 'old school tie' just didn't seem to cut it anymore.

---

[19] David Kynaston and Francis Green, *Engines of Privilege, Britain's Private School Problem*, Bloomsbury Publishing, London, 2019.

[20] Until 2008, a typical High Court judge had to have about 20 to 30 years' experience as a lawyer.

[21] The former Premier of the Australian State of New South Wales (NSW) Jack Lang, famously once said, 'In the race of life, always back self-interest—at least you know it's trying.'

[22] David Cameron constantly had to defend his 'fantastic school' and often repeated that, 'It's not where you've come from that counts most, it's where you're going'. He put up with continual criticism, even derision, about the excessive numbers of privately educated Cabinet members and upper-class appointments at No.10. The derision even came from his own party. Sir John Major, who left grammar school just before his 16th birthday and succeeded Margaret Thatcher as

In the 1980s, public schools, all registered as charities, reinvented themselves as businesses, going global, searching out the children of the world's super-rich. Harrow, for example, was one of the first public schools to expand abroad when it opened Harrow International Bangkok. Since then, it has established branches in Hong Kong, Beijing, and Shanghai. Cashed up public schools now enjoy resources that are about three times greater per pupil than the average state school.

The advantages of a private education to those who can afford it are obvious (causing rich parents to rush out to put their child's name down at birth, even conception): intergenerational continuity, history and tradition, a disciplined and dignified environment, a positive, individualised and motivating learning experience, more and better qualified teachers, a culture of innovation, considerably smaller class sizes, an upper-class English accent, social graces, and an exclusive peer group. And last, but not at all least—and the real name of the game—a high percentage of A level results (compared to the comprehensive school system), and then perceived access to both established and informal networks. And this would have been in the minds of Bill Roache's parents too.

Conservative Prime Minister in 1990, said it was 'truly shocking' in November 2013; his education secretary Michael Gove said it was 'preposterous' and 'ridiculous'; and Baroness Warsi said those around Cameron were 'public schoolboys'. His successor Theresa May made popular anti-privilege speeches and appointed a meritocratic Cabinet with less than a quarter of privately educated ministers, only to be succeeded by another old Etonian Boris Johnson in 2019.

Still, as in Bill Roache's day, the stubborn fact remains that the main conflict in the debate is social inequality versus freedom of choice especially when, even today, 93% of the population do not have the means to exercise that same freedom. Freedom, after all, is not about what you choose but what can be chosen.

On a very positive note, today a vital part of the Rydal Penrhos School's work is to administer the Donald Hughes Trust. This provides fully funded places based on academic merit alone. There is also a bursaries programme, which helps with fees and makes awards based on academic achievement or contributions to the sporting or artistic life of the school. The trust is named after the former head of Rydal School, who would pay the fees for children out of his own pocket if they were at risk of losing their places.

Our spirited reflections aside, the important question now is, in what ways did a public school education contribute to the making of Bill Roache? And as a future chapter will explore, what positive foundations did Rydal lay for his remarkable future career in acting?

As for cold school baths, something public school boys never seem to forget, he later commented,

It was hell. Far from building my character and making me a hardy member of the British Empire, it turned me into a hothouse plant who won't swim unless the pool is steaming, and whose central heating is kept on all year.

And being forced to use his right hand?

I would get things the wrong way around, like writing the number '9' instead of the letter 'P'. This got to the point where whole words would be written back to front. In one essay, for example, I used the word 'god' instead of 'dog'. Hopefully, I have been forgiven the blasphemy, and I suspect it made the piece more interesting to read anyway.

Notwithstanding the Rydal matron's strategy to save hot water, Bill has described his childhood as mostly 'free and casual' and largely defined by time spent on his own—which he says was a consequence of boarding school where he did not see his school chums in the holidays and didn't have the opportunity to make local friends. (He did, however, learn to play canasta at Rydal, which after all, is a card game usually played by four in two partnerships.)

Above all, what boarding school seems to have done for Bill Roache is to give him a sense of personal self-sufficiency, including the practical skills necessary to be able to look after himself and enjoy his own company, which is something that very much defines him today. (Bill describes his dressing room at Granada Television studios in Manchester, as well as his home conservatory, as 'sanctuaries' where he can be utterly alone with only his thoughts for company.) And Bill is very clear that a public school education helped him adjust to the discipline of army life. As he says,

I was already used to being away from my family and fitting in wherever I went. This time, though, I was known as 22626311 Fusilier Roache rather than Fish.[23]

And, although the adjudicator at the Rydal School music competition advised young Bill to 'Stick to rugby and forget the trumpet', the trumpet (a solo instrument) had become a metaphor for his later life. As Bill says,

Taking up the trumpet, what does that tell you? A single instrument blasting out—you can't get more individualistic than that! I was beginning to want to stand out in some way.

---

[23] 'Fish' was Bill Roache's nickname at Rydal.

CHAPTER FOUR

National Service and the Regular Army
22626311 Fusilier Roache, Sir!

In his book *Merchant, Soldier, Sage: A New History of Power* (2012), David Priestland proposes that three 'castes' predominate throughout society, and each is driven by differing value systems—the commercial and competitive (merchant), the aristocratic and militaristic (soldier), and the bureaucratic or creative (sage). This theory focuses on these differing value systems and traces how they operate within society. If we are to accept the idea that we are all driven by one of these systems, what happens when the state demands that a 'sage' becomes a 'soldier'?

On 3 January 1952, 19-year-old Bill Roache was called up for his two years of National Service and reported to the Depot of The Royal Welch Fusiliers at Hightown Barracks, Wrexham in Clwyd, North Wales.[1]

---

[1] The Regiment is said to have retained the archaic spelling of 'Welch' first used around 1700, however, from 1881 until 1921 the War Office

Here he became 22626311 Fusilier Roache, Sir!

The Royal Welch Fusiliers was one of the most distinguished regiments of the British Army. It was raised in 1689 under King William III and had seen service around the world. It was one of the six Minden Regiments that had halted the French cavalry during the Seven Years' War (1756–1763); it had served in the American Revolutionary War (1775–1783) from Lexington to Yorktown (where it was the only British regiment not to surrender its colours); it had seen service under the Duke of Wellington during the Peninsular War in Spain (1811) and at Waterloo (1815), during the Crimean War (1854), the Indian Mutiny (1857), the Second Opium War in China (1856–1860) and the Third Anglo-Burmese War (1885).

During World War One (The Great War, 1914–1918), it had raised the fourth highest number of battalions of any regiment on the Army List (40), and, in both World Wars, it had been represented in every theatre of operations. As well as a fearsome military record, it also boasted an unrivalled literary and artistic heritage dating from the American War, although its most famous sons were the Great War poets such as Robert Graves, David Jones, Siegfried Sassoon and Hedd Wyn (who wrote in Welsh). More recently, its ranks included the actors Andrew Cruikshank (Dr Cameron in *Dr Finlay's Casebook*), Jack Hawkins (*The Cruel Sea and Bridge over the River Kwai*),

---

insisted that the spelling be 'The Royal Welsh Fusiliers'. 'Welch' continued to be used informally until restored in 1920 by Army Order No.56.

John Kidd (*Doomwatch*), Desmond Llewellyn ('Q' in the James Bond franchise) and André Morell (Professor Bernard Quatermass in Q*uatermass and the Pit*), in whose footsteps Bill was to follow. (In the First World War the Regiment was known for its writers, in the Second World War it was the actors!)

The Regiment boasted several peculiarities of dress and custom. The officers and men wore the Flash, a bunch of black ribbons on the back of the collar—the last remnant of the pigtail—the non-commissioned ranks wore the White Hackle, a feathered plume held behind the cap badge; in full dress, the bearskin or sealskin was proudly worn by junior ranks. Every battalion had included on its strength a goat, never 'a mascot', and always named 'Billy'—a physical reminder of Welsh identity, which in the case of the 1st and 2nd Battalions was drawn from the Royal herd.

Welsh identity was most evident in the celebration of St. David's Day, 1 March, which the 1st Battalion was unable to keep on only one occasion—during the Burma campaign (1944–1945). Like all regiments, it was a close-knit family in which sons followed fathers, and the network of brothers, cousins and in-laws was part of the glue that held the Regiment together.

At Hightown Barracks, the standard fare for a recruit included a medical examination, a haircut (more like a shaved convict), the issue of 'kit', the personal equipment carried by the common soldier, going everywhere 'at the double', and then learning how to 'swab, scrub and shine', to 'bull and blanco', and to lay out beds and gear all under the watchful eye of a senior trained soldier or corporal. 'Bulling,' 'bull polishing', 'spit polishing' or 'spit shining' are terms commonly used by British soldiers and refer to a method for polishing leather.[2]

However, what brought home to Bill the reality of army life—more than the issue of a uniform, or going around in a squad, or breaking in a pair of unyielding new ammunition boots, or even the forceful language of the sergeants—was the possession of a rifle, a bolt action .303 Lee-Enfield and bayonet, the basic tools of an infantry soldier at the time. The Lee–Enfield takes its name from the designer of the rifle's bolt system James Paris Lee and the factory in which it was designed—the Royal Small Arms Factory in Enfield, North London.[3]

Thereafter, with the rest of his platoon of 30 men, Bill was transformed from a civilian into a trained soldier. For the first six weeks, life was defined by the confines of Hightown Barracks and the barrack room in Ellis block where he slept. He soon became aware of what a leveller

---

[2] Blanco is a compound used by service men and women throughout the Commonwealth from 1880 onwards to clean and colour equipment. Colours include tan, two shades of green—including khaki, the Hindustani word for 'dust'—black, white for the navy and blue for the airforce.

[3] The Pattern 1907 bayonet was officially called the Sword bayonet, pattern 1907 (Mark I). One of the manufacturers was the British company Wilkinson Sword who also make shaving razors and more recently gardening equipment.

National Service was. There were old Etonians and university graduates rubbing shoulders with working-class men, some of whom could neither read nor write—and on more than one occasion needed Bill's assistance to correspond home. When basic training was near its end, and the platoon could handle weapons, shoot, and drill smartly, there was time for the odd evening in town. At the end of it, the platoon passed off the square with enough credit to be chosen as the escort to the Regimental Colours at Wrexham Town Hall, where the mayor announced the accession of the young Queen Elizabeth II to the throne.

The next step in training took place at the Welsh Brigade training depot at Brecon where Bill Roache and his platoon joined around 300 other soldiers undergoing advanced combat training. Here, fate intervened to stop him completing his National Service as a fusilier or possibly a non-commissioned officer. Having the School Certificate, he was picked to attend selection for officer training at the War Office Selection Board. As Bill relates in his autobiography, *Ken and Me*, he went on for further training at Eaton Hall Officer Cadet Training Unit.

His arrival was not auspicious for, as he recounts, he committed the worst crime possible in the eyes of a drill sergeant—not merely riding his motorcycle across the 'sacred' parade ground but riding it between the sergeant and the troops he was drilling! Hauled in front of his company commander before he had even begun his first day, he felt that his career as an officer might be over before it had even started. Fortunately, his company commander had a sense of humour. His reprimand consisted of, 'You won't do it again, will you, Roache?' Bill went on to complete his training, commissioned into the Royal Welch Fusiliers as Second-Lieutenant W.P. Roache.

Bill assumed, with understandable dread, that he would join either the 2nd Battalion on operations in Malaya, or the 1st Battalion on operations in the Korean War. However, kindly fate once again intervened, as the war had reached stalemate and the 2nd Battalion was fully manned. Instead, he had the pleasant surprise of being posted to far sunnier climes.

In January 1953, Bill joined the Regiment's 1st Battalion, 1 R.W.F., in Jamaica, where the British military presence in the Caribbean was based. Jamaica had been a British colony since its acquisition by Oliver Cromwell in 1655. There was only one regular infantry battalion stationed in the region but other military forces included the locally recruited Jamaica Battalion, as well as the Volunteer Guards in British Honduras, British Guiana, Trinidad and Tobago, the Leeward Islands, and the Windward Islands.

The British battalion was based at Up Park Camp, Kingston, with a 'change-of-air' outstation at Newcastle in the hills, 18 miles away and 3,700 feet above sea level. Newcastle was established as a military centre in the 1840s by then Major-General Sir William Maynard Gomm, Lieutenant-Governor of Jamaica and Britain's longest serving soldier. Before 1948, a company-sized detachment of about 100 men was established in British Honduras (now Belize) as a deterrent to Guatemalan invasion; it was withdrawn in that year but, in December 1953, Prime Minister Winston Churchill announced that the garrison would be re-established. The British battalion was responsible for providing troops for internal security and other duties throughout the area, including ceremonial parades, guards of honour and escorts. The pace of life, however, was far from hectic.

In the Caribbean, 1 R.W.F. was always a low priority for manpower, not least because the 2nd Battalion of the Regiment was being prepared for service, first in Korea and later in Malaya. National Service meant that there was a constant turnover of trained men, whose loss was felt particularly badly in the platoons' Support Company where the Battalion's heavy weapons—mortars, machine guns and anti-tank guns—were centralised. Because of the shortage of manpower, only three of the four rifle companies, A, B and D, could be manned. C Company posted its men to the other rifle companies and became a training company located at Newcastle where, as well as going on courses, the men and their families could take short leave to enjoy the cooler climate.

Bill joined B Company under Major Guy Tolhurst and Company Sergeant-Major Oscar Slater,[4] both veterans

---

[4] Oscar Slater was a veteran of the Battle of Kohima, in which he lost the tip of his nose to a Japanese bullet during one of several ill-fated attempts to capture Kuki Piquet. The battle was the turning point in the Japanese U-Go offensive into British India. The battle took place in three stages from 4 April to 22 June 1944 around the town of Kohima, now the capital of Nagaland, northeast India.

of the Second World War. Tolhurst was, as Bill recorded, not very interested in his profession, and appeared to be serving out his time before retirement. Slater, by contrast, was a tough soldier who was dedicated to his profession and to the Regiment. The company was short of men and, as a result, the only platoon was being commanded by its other subaltern, Selwyn Hughes, with whom Bill rapidly became close friends.

Up Park Camp consisted of wooden bungalows raised on pillars about three feet above the ground. This allowed air to circulate and discouraged insects and snakes. It boasted a good rifle range and opportunities for sport. Polo was of special interest to the Commanding Officer, Lieutenant-Colonel J.R. (Jimmy) Johnson. Johnson had joined the Regiment before the Second World War, when the main preoccupations of Royal Welch Fusilier officers were hunting, shooting, racing, cricket, and especially polo. Johnson was a keen player himself and insisted that as many officers as possible should participate. Bill had a narrow escape, as he was left-handed.[5]

Johnson was a formidable soldier having been with the 1st Battalion in the dreadful battles around St. Venant, France in 1940. Of the 700 members of the Royal Welch Fusiliers who defended the village, only five officers and 263 other ranks managed to reach the beachhead at

---

[5] The banning of left-handed players, or more correctly, playing left-handed, was enforced to avoid the head-on collision of a left-handed player and a right-handed player while simultaneously approaching the ball 'and falling foul of the offside rule'.

Dunkirk where they were evacuated on 31 May. Johnson had been captured by the Germans but had escaped and made the only 'home run' by a regimental officer during the Second World War, for which he was awarded the Military Cross (MC).[6] Bill described his first meeting with Johnson, who was dressed in Bermuda shorts, a flowery shirt, and sandals—not at all what he had come to expect of a senior officer.

1 RWF had arrived by troopship on 19 March 1951 and had despatched companies by air for various tasks such as restoring civil order in Grenada in May 1951, and garrison duties in British Honduras. In August 1951, a hurricane struck Jamaica and the Battalion was heavily engaged in relief operations throughout the months of August and September. The death of the King and the Proclamation of the new Queen in early 1952 had been significant events, not least because the monarch was also Colonel-in-Chief of the Regiment.

The cost of living in Jamaica was high because of import duties. Bill's basic pay as a Lieutenant was £1/3s/6d (£1.17) per day, or about £36 per month—around £900 at today's rates. Extra messing charges of 2/6d (12 1/2p) per day were levied out of this and, as an example of a basic commodity, soap cost 1/3d (6p) per bar, or £1.59 at today's rates. All this was partly offset by a local overseas allowance of 2/3d

---

[6] We are indebted to Timandra Slade for her research in this field. Timandra Slade, *From a Hard Place to a Rock: Firsthand Accounts of Soldiers of the British Expeditionary Force on the Run in World War Two*, Troubador Publishing, London, 2022.

(11p) per day, about £1 at today's prices. Alcohol, however, was cheap, and readily available. Bill recalled rum at 2d a tot, and Red Stripe Jamaican brewed beer and Tom Collins cocktails—the cause of many a hangover.[7]

The local brothels were also inexpensive and in heavy demand by the fusiliers; in fact, the Battalion medical officer told Bill that anything up to 70% of an infantry battalion might expect to contract some form of venereal disease during their tour of the West Indies. Leave was a problem in the early days, since resorts like Montego Bay were beyond the means of most and returning to Britain was prohibitively expensive and slow. The solution was the establishment of a leave camp at Port Antonio on the north coast, which proved very popular.

In July 1952, troopships ceased to operate on the Atlantic run and air trooping was introduced on a regular basis, flights being operated twice monthly by Skyways Ltd. The flight was a long one, via Iceland, Gander airport in Newfoundland, and Bermuda. As Bill described, unlike regular airliners, the Hudson converted bomber that Bill was on only flew at 8,500 feet above the cold, stormy Atlantic. Even so, it was easier than the long voyage by troopship unless, as happened to Bill, mechanical failure led to long layovers along the air route.

Just after he arrived in 1953, air trooping resulted in a disaster for the Battalion. On 2 February, a York aircraft

---

[7] A Tom Collins is traditionally made from gin, lemon juice, sugar and carbonated water served in a Collins glass over ice.

carrying reinforcements and families from Britain crashed off the Newfoundland coast with the loss of all 39 people on board. The cause of the accident was never discovered, nor were any bodies or wreckage ever found.[8]

On 1 March 1953, Bill enjoyed his first celebration of St. David's Day. There was a Drumhead ceremony (a religious service attended by members of a military unit while in the field) at which the Governor handed over four silver bugles that had been purchased by the officers and sergeants for the Corps of Drums. It was at this time that Bill Roache and Selwyn Hughes were overtaken by a series of disasters: thinking they had overslept and then being ready for parade two hours early; being caught out in the wrong position on parade and being persecuted by ants crawling over their faces.

The Governor, Sir Hugh Foot (later Baron Caradon)— brother of Michael Foot (leader of the UK Labour Party 1980–1983)—and Dingle Foot (a Liberal and later Labour politician) joined the officers for their formal dinner, at which Bill 'ate the leek,' standing on his chair with one foot on the table while a drummer played a drum role, then drinking a draught of champagne from a silver loving cup

---

[8] The Royal Welch lost Sergeant and Mrs Gwyn Busst with their two children, a three-year-old boy, Colin and a baby boy, Trevor; Corporals Sydney Glaze and David Baker; Bandsman and Mrs Donald Platt; Fusilier Bill Jones; Mrs Margaret Tierney and her two children, a three-year-old girl, Linda, and a baby boy, Dale; Mrs Moira Vaughan and her two-year-old son, Bernard; Corporal and Mrs Horace Bayliss and their daughter, Lesley; and Mrs Violet James.

to the toast, *'and Saint David!'* [9] This was an unvarying rite of passage for any young officer joining the Regiment and marked his acceptance into the family.

Just before Coronation week in 1953, 1 R.W.F. was warned to provide 250 men, the Regimental band, drums, and pioneers to go to Bermuda for security and ceremonial duties during three-power talks between the governments of Great Britain, France, and the US.[10]

A major task during the first half of that year was a series of duties connected with the forthcoming Coronation of Queen Elizabeth II. The first of these was the organisation of the Jamaica Coronation Tattoo, preparations for which started early in the spring and went on until June. Besides the Battalion, the tattoo involved 250 men of the Jamaica Battalion, 400 Scouts, 300 Cadets, 350 schoolchildren, 120 civilians and 200 members of the Jamaica Constabulary.

The tattoo was held between 2 and 8 June and was considered an unqualified success, being enjoyed by over 75,000 people. Two additional performances were held by popular demand. Bill's job was to organise the nightly fireworks display, an assignment which nearly came to grief, when his assistant, one Sergeant Duffissey, got drunk—'Smashed out of his mind on Red Stripe lager,'

---

[9] Meaning to be compelled to take back one's words or put up with insulting treatment (from the scene between Fluellen and Pistol in Shakespeare's *Henry V*).

[10] It was also Prime Minister (by then Sir Winston) Churchill's 'wish' that the Regimental Goat be present.

according to Bill. But by good luck and considerable energy, Second-Lieutenant W.P. Roache saved the day.

Suddenly, a spray of sparks spluttered out of the first rocket. Simultaneously, Sergeant Duffissey staggered backwards, knocking it sideways. The sparks and fire shot down the whole length of the ramp, igniting in one go all the rockets for the entire display. Seeing this I dashed around and lit every one of the fireworks as quickly as possible to preserve some kind of sequence. The display intended to last ten minutes was over in two. Having established that Sergeant Duffissey, apart from being drunk, was in good health, I slumped despondently on the grass in my scorched shirt. Then the Colonel came running over to me. Oh, God, I thought, now I'm in for it and stood up to face the tirade. "Well done, Mr Roache," he exclaimed. "Smashing. Haven't enjoyed myself so much for ages. Keep it up!" So, a ten-minute display became a two-minute display for the remaining three days.

On 4 September 1953, B Company moved to Moneague Camp, followed by the main body of the Battalion. By now, B Company had enough manpower for Bill to have a command of his own, a small platoon of about 20 men. Here it was intended to carry out some training, a welcome relief from the endless round of fatigue duties, parades, and guards in Kingston. The Battalion returned to Up Park Camp on 29 September and was ordered to move at very short notice for internal security duties in

British Guiana. It was at this time that Bill left B Company and took over the Battalion's 3-inch Mortar Platoon.

The orders directed 1 R.W.F. to proceed with the utmost speed to British Guiana where serious disorder seemed imminent. A new government under Cheddi Berret Jagan had been elected following the introduction of a new constitution. Ominously, Jagan had publicly praised the Mau Mau rebels in Kenya for the killing of Europeans. The British Government ordered troops to the area to support the Governor. On 3 October, under the cover of an elaborate deception story in the Caribbean press, B Company, now without Bill, embarked on H.M.S. *Bigbury Bay*. On 4 October, the remainder of the Battalion embarked from an oil jetty at Trinidad Leaseholds' wharf in the cruiser H.M.S. *Superb*.

B Company, now under Major J.M. Neill, was escorted by mounted police guides, marched by platoons in anti-riot box formation with fixed bayonets, from the docks to the Eve Leary parade ground, dropping a platoon at Government House to mount guard. The remainder marched on without incident, to be met with a welcome breakfast by the British Guiana Volunteer Guard. The rest of the officers and men and all the stores came ashore throughout the day, during which the most pressing problem identified was billeting. This was solved by taking over two hotels—the Carib and the Bel Air—and two sports clubs, putting an end to social life in the capital. Bill, who remained behind, found his time taken up with patrols along the coast roads, demonstrations of force and parade. There was no sign of violence, although a popular local calypso in five verses was sung, to which the chorus was:

> *Go home, go home, Bigbury Bay,*
> *Welsh Fusilier, you cannot stay.*
> *Go home to British Admiralty,*
> *And let us live in democracy.*

On 13 October, operations were stepped up to include the mounting of roadblocks and patrols, assistance to the police, and house searches throughout the colony. The officers and men were, however, allowed to walk out unarmed when off duty; Bill and several others even managed to go on a shoot. This almost ended in disaster when an alligator, which had supposedly been shot dead, came back to life in their canoe. Ten days later, 1 R.W.F. was relieved by the Argyll and Sutherland Highlanders and embarked an old bauxite ship, the S.S. *Sunjarv*, for the return trip to Jamaica.

The final ceremonial event of the Coronation year was The Queen's visit to Jamaica during the Commonwealth tour. On 25 November, Her Majesty, accompanied by the Duke of Edinburgh, landed at Montego Bay, and drove by the north coast road and Mount Diablo to Kingston. The Battalion lined the streets of Spanish Town, the old capital of Jamaica. The next day, the whole garrison turned out for The Queen, the parade concluding with an impressive *feu de joie*—a salute fired by every man on parade in succession along the ranks to make one continuous sound.

(During the Diamond Jubilee of *Coronation Street* in 2021, Her Majesty visited the show's set and studios and was greeted by Bill Roache as the most senior cast member. He took the opportunity to inform The Queen that he had seen her when she visited Jamaica in 1953.)

That evening, a representative party from the Battalion met the Colonel-in-Chief at a reception at King's House, among whom was the Regimental Goat which was rewarded with a royal cigarette washed down with a gin sling, compliments of Lady Pamela Mountbatten. As soon as The Queen's visit was concluded, the 240-strong detachment returned to Bermuda by air to resume their interrupted duty at the Anglo-American French inter-governmental conference.

Guards were found for the arrival of Sir Winston Churchill at Kinley Field on 2 December, Monsieur Laniel the French Prime Minister on 3 December, and President Eisenhower on 4 December. There was a story circulating at the time of difficulties in getting the goat from Jamaica to Bermuda because of animal health regulations and transport problems. It is said that the knotted red tape was cut by a typically abrupt telegram from Winston Churchill which simply said, 'Fumigate the animal and fly it.' It was reported that the goat enjoyed himself no end in Bermuda, being rewarded at a state banquet with a cigarette from the British Prime Minister and a glass of champagne from the American President. Only the French Premier did not appreciate the goat, with the Parisian newspaper *Combat* reporting,

Churchill ignored Monsieur Laniel while the two men were waiting to greet Eisenhower … instead he [Churchill] spent his time ostentatiously caressing the goat of the Guard of Honour at the airport.

Bill, however, had seen the last of Jamaica, as he was sent home to attend a training course on the three-inch mortar where he was later to sustain permanent hearing damage in a training accident.[11] His Christmas was spent on a banana boat—attending a party that he described as 'magical'. New Year was spent with his family, before he went to the Small Arms School at Hythe in Kent where, after his explosive 'adventures,' he rejoined 1 R.W.F., which had returned to Britain for a short period after farewell celebrations in Jamaica.

These festivities were something of a test of Bill's now renowned stamina. On 16 February, the Governor gave a dinner for some of the officers; a Farewell Retreat ceremony was held at Up Park Camp on 17 February at which the Prime Minister of Jamaica, Mr Bustamante, took the salute; the Liguanea Club gave a farewell dance

---

[11] Bill's account is, 'I was put in charge of the 3-inch Mortar Platoon. We were on a training course, firing live ammunition. After I loaded the bomb, it didn't detonate. So, the guy behind me over-enthusiastically pulled the weapon upright and it then went off, with my head above the line of the mortar. I got the full blast in both ears. I couldn't hear at all for two weeks. But in those days, you were stoical. I thought it would pass and after two weeks my hearing did go back to what I thought was normal, but it wasn't. If I'd reported it, or gone to the medical centre at the time, I'd probably be on some great Army pension now.'

on 19 February and on 20 February 'Taffy's Ball' was held, which was also a farewell party for the Commanding Officer. Three days later, on 23 February, Lieutenant-Colonel Johnson handed over command to Lieutenant-Colonel Neville Bosanquet; St. David's Day was celebrated on 1 March and, on 5 March, a second farewell in the form of a march through the streets was held, at the request of the Mayor of Kingston. The Battalion's long and diverse spell of duty in the West Indies ended on 11 March 1954, when it embarked at Kingston on the H.M. Troopship *Empire Clyde*.

When 1 R.W.F. left Jamaica, it did not go directly to its new station in Germany but rather to Chiseldon Camp, near Marlborough in Wiltshire where all three battalions of the Regiment—the 1st, 2nd and 4th were to go on parade to receive new Stands of Colours from their Colonel-in-Chief, the young Queen Elizabeth II. Bill was selected for a very particular honour on this parade—to carry the old Regimental Colour of the 1st Battalion for the last time as it was marched off parade after 66 years of service.

The 1st Battalion arrived at Chiseldon in Wiltshire on 26 March 1954 and was soon joined at nearby Ogbourne St. George by the 2nd Battalion under Lieutenant-Colonel 'Winky' Benyon. The 4th Battalion, which was a territorial unit, would start its camp on 11 July. The ceremony was fixed for 23 July. It was decided to use Wroughton airfield for the ceremony rather than Tidworth Arena, because the airfield was close by, making administration simple; it was big enough to take the parade, and offered plenty of hard standing ground. There was also covered accommodation in the event of bad weather. It proved an excellent choice.

The weather forecast for 23 July was indifferent but the airfield Met Office suggested local conditions would be reasonably safe. It was therefore decided early that morning that the parade would go ahead outside. The parade was led by the Massed Bands and Corps of Drums, halting in front of the saluting base and the great mass of spectators who had come from all over Wales—and many other parts of the world—to see the event. The parade was so large that a line of double guards was formed. The silver drums of the 2nd Battalion were then piled, and the new Colours laid on them. All was then ready, and the parade awaited The Queen's arrival. Benyon later recalled,

> *Suddenly it seemed there on the saluting base, amongst us, dressed all in white, was the slight figure of The Colonel-in-Chief. The Royal Salute crashed out and I must confess that I felt proud indeed as I reported to Her Majesty, Your Royal Welch Fusiliers are present and ready for your inspection. There are 101 officers and 1,006 other ranks on parade.*

After the inspection, carried out from a Land Rover, the old Colours of the 1st and 4th Battalions were trooped through the ranks and marched off for the last time with Bill carrying the Regimental Colour of the 1st Battalion. The consecration of the new Colours was carried out and then presented to each battalion in turn, after which Her Majesty addressed the Regiment with these words,

It is a moving experience to watch old Colours being marched off parade for the last time. Into their faded fabric is woven the story of notable feats of bravery and endurance in the field and many a record of faithful service at home and overseas. They are carried away to be laid up, accompanied by the loyalty and affection of all who have served under them ... I entrust these new Colours into your safe-keeping, confident that you will jealously preserve them and the distinctive traditions of The Royal Welch Fusiliers which they symbolise.

Lieutenant-Colonel Benyon replied briefly on behalf of the Regiment. The parade then marched past by battalion, re-formed, advanced in review order, gave a Royal Salute and then three cheers for Her Majesty. Benyon then received permission to march off. While this was going on, a large body of Old Comrades formed up and were inspected by Her Majesty after the conclusion of the parade.

The presentation was followed by a reception and luncheon. When Her Majesty left, the route through the camp was lined by men of all battalions and many hundreds of spectators, Bill among them. That evening, celebrations were held, including a cocktail party, dinners, and a ball, where a telegram of congratulations was received from Buckingham Palace.

Not long afterwards, 1 R.W.F. was posted to Germany, to join the British Army of the Rhine. The unit completed its move to Moore Barracks, Dortmund, on 15 August

1954. Dortmund lies at the eastern extremity of the Ruhr industrial zone. The Battalion was organised into Battalion HQ and HQ Company; four rifle companies, of which D Company was initially a cadre company responsible for training and for handling drafts; and a support company of 3-inch mortar, anti-tank, machine-gun, and pioneer platoons—Bill Roache was in command of the Mortar Platoon. The manning situation improved greatly during the early months of 1955 but, although Battalion strength rose to nearly 1,000 across all ranks, there was always a shortage of officers, particularly Majors and Captains, largely due to the Regiment fielding two regular battalions, one of which was on operations in Malaya.

The Battalion was immediately committed to brigade, divisional, and theatre-level training: these were the first exercises above company level in which the Battalion had participated since the late summer of 1950. Given the large turnover of national servicemen, it was already a substantially different battalion from that which had left the West Indies. Exercises *Rebirth* and *Two Keys* were held between 6 and 11 September and were followed by exercise *Battle Royal* from 19 to 27 September which was, ominously, in a nuclear war scenario.

A traditional Christmas was celebrated in very cold weather with early morning 'gunfire'—tea heavily laced with rum, and dinner served by the officers and senior NCOs, including Bill. A lucky incident at the time made for great progress in relations with the local people. The press reported that the Battalion was giving a party for

German children and a little German girl wrote asking whether she could come too. A letter was sent back saying that really the party was for the children of the Battalion's own workers, but as she had written such a nice letter, Santa Claus would like her to join in. The girl's story was written up in both the British and German newspapers to great approval. As a result, the Battalion was flooded with invitations to spend Christmas and New Year with German families and more than 50 men enjoyed a traditional Yuletide celebration.

Training resumed immediately after Christmas with exercise *Dolly Drop* in January 1955 and exercise *Longlegs* in February. One officer calculated that, out of 273 days, he had spent 104 nights on training. It was not surprising then that Bill did not enjoy this hard, repetitive, regimental soldiering. His comment was, 'I realised how lucky I'd been to have been posted to Jamaica.' He further said, 'I was growing bored and restless.' And as a result, he disobeyed the oldest military maxim in the book and volunteered for something. In this case, it was for service as a British officer in command of Arab troops in the Trucial Oman Scouts. Bill left Germany for the sunnier climes of the Arabian Peninsula and never saw his old Battalion again.

CHAPTER FIVE
Law and Life Lessons
Follow the Yellow Brick Road?

During the celebrated 1980s *Coronation Street* break up of Ken and Deirdre Barlow ('*Coronation Street's* Richard Burton and Elizabeth Taylor'), there was a line of scripted dialogue that was unexpectedly to change the course of Bill Roache's life—first for the worse and then, for his personal and spiritual development—for the very best.

The fateful words were a small part of a *Coronation Street* storyline that lasted the best part of a decade. The dialogue in question was a seemingly throwaway line. Exasperated, Ken confronted his on-screen wife Deirdre (Anne Kirkbride) with the purely rhetorical question, 'You think I'm boring, don't you?' Almost instantly, 'Boring Barlow' appeared in headlines in newspapers and magazines everywhere—and the alliteration stuck. The television critics had a field day. In fact, it gave the press something new to write about—especially *The Sun* and especially Ken Irwin, the same journalist who wrote in 1960 that *Coronation Street* 'would not last a week'.

Under the ownership of News Corp and the editorship of Kelvin MacKenzie, *The Sun*[1] gained a reputation for sensationalist and sometimes completely fabricated stories, including the memorable front page headline FREDDIE STARR ATE MY HAMSTER (13 March 1986).[2] In the late 1980s alone, the paper was served with 17 libel writs including one by Sir Elton John who *The Sun* claimed—amongst other more salacious and untrue allegations—had his Rottweiler guard dogs' voice boxes surgically removed to stop them annoying a neighbour. The canine-loving British public were outraged. (John's dogs were actually Alsatians and they continued to enjoy a good bark despite *The Sun's* rabid headlines.) The 1987 case never made it to trial. Rather, Sir Elton was advised to accept an out-of-court settlement, together with the front-page headline retraction: SORRY ELTON. And he agreed. It was the largest damages settlement in British history.

In 2018, *The Sun on Sunday* was at it again—a glutton for punishment—with a story that untruthfully claimed that a child on a play date at the home of Sir Elton and David Furnish, together with their two sons, was attacked by Sir Elton's dog and left with 'Freddy Krueger-like injuries'. The story was republished by the *Mail Online*, the *Metro*, the *Daily Mirror*, and the *Evening Standard*. The newspaper

---

[1] *The Sun* is published in the UK as a tabloid and in the Republic of Ireland as a broadsheet.
[2] When Freddie Starr (born Frederick Leslie Fowell) died (1943–2019), *The Sun's* front page headline was FREDDIE STARR JOINS HIS HAMSTER.

(part of the News Group Newspapers) was forced to 'unequivocally accept that the allegation was false,' agree to 'pay significant damages, and reimburse the couple's legal costs').

For Bill Roache, Elton John's 1987 case should have been a cautionary reminder of what the American author Mark Twain once said, 'The public is the only critic whose opinion is worth anything at all'—because, as an actor, Bill's profile with a global television audience was unquestioned. He was later to write that fate in the form of a chance meeting with Ken Irwin (queuing for the same Manchester-bound train at Euston Station, London) presented him with an opportunity to 'let it go and to move on', but instead, he chose the tortuous path of litigation, ultimately learning a costly lesson about pride and ego—and most importantly for him, forgiveness.

The details of the case are well known. In November 1990, *The Sun*—at that time Britain's largest circulation daily, published a series of articles written by Ken Irwin, the self-styled 'friend of "The Street"'.[3] According to Bill, the two-page feature published on 1 November 1990 about him was mostly, 'demeaning and unsubstantiated gossip' presented as fact. 'Nothing more than personal and poisonous opinion'—exactly what *The Sun* was known for and what many of their readers had come to expect.

Bill had not given Ken Irwin an interview for the article—and this was confirmed by the *Coronation Street* press

---

[3] Circulation was overtaken by rival *Metro* in 2018.

officer later in court; rather the story was attributed to 'anonymous sources' and 'unnamed insiders'. According to Bill, it wasn't a celebration of his contribution at all—but rather a calculated character assassination centred around false allegations that he—'Roache' (as Ken Irwin referred to him in the article)—'was nearly fired on several occasions, was hated by the cast and was as dull and smug in real life as his fictional character', a point tediously reinforced by the reverberating tabloid echo of 'Boring Ken Barlow!'

Humiliated, Bill engaged one of the UK's leading libel lawyers, who advised him of an '80% chance of success'. *The Sun* initially declined an invitation to pay his costs and print a public apology as it had done with Sir Elton. The hearing was scheduled for 29 October 1991—almost a year after the article first went to press: *William Roache v. News Group Newspapers Ltd, Kelvin MacKenzie (editor) and Ken Irwin (journalist).*

To say that Bill was motivated by greed would be to misrepresent his purpose in pursuing the case. Rather, his position was,

> *My brush with the press and the legal system opened my eyes to a great injustice which I believe must be put right … misinformation, bias and lies affect the functioning of our democracy. Because for a democracy to work properly people must be accurately and honestly informed …*

Bill was ahead of his time in holding Fleet Street to account for printing what has become known as 'fake news', as well as defending the importance of quality journalism.[4] It was to take another ten years for a police enquiry to convict a News UK journalist (the company that published *The Sun*) for intercepting the phone messages of members of the Royal staff and some 20 years for the Independent Police Complaints Commission Operation Elveden to secure a conviction against another News UK journalist for 'aiding and abetting misconduct in public office', namely making payment to a police officer in exchange for information. Significantly, the trial judge, His Honour Timothy Pontius, said in court that the latter had been, 'clearly recognised procedure at *The Sun*.'[5]

For this reason—precisely on a matter of principle—the defendant's first offer of £25,000, called a Part 36 offer under the Civil Procedure Rules, was rejected out of hand by Bill's legal team. According to him, the amount simply did not provide a deterrent to future bad behaviour on the part of *The Sun*. The records show that Bill was aware at the time that, if he took the money, *The Sun* would apologise, pay his costs and the case would not proceed.

---

[4] 'Fake news' is fabricated, false, misleading, or non-verifiable content presented as legitimate reportage. The term has been broadened, and even 'weaponised' by some, to include all news that presents a so-called 'negative' or analytical view.

[5] In 2020, Prince Harry began advocating for objective and truthful reporting while defending himself and his wife Meghan, Duchess of Sussex, against sections of the British press who he said were 'waging campaigns against individuals with no thought as to the consequences'.

He was also advised that, if he did not accept the money and the case went to court and he was awarded damages of the same amount (or less) then he would have to pay the costs of both sides.

In October of that year, News Group increased the sum paid into court to £50,000. The case proceeded with fate taking its inevitable disastrous course. While details of the case are on the public record, what may not be well understood for a person embarking on a course of litigation in the UK is the very difficult decision a claimant like Bill Roache has to make on the question of costs when a Part 36 offer is made. This is because costs can dwarf any award of damages and lead to financial ruin for the claimant.

Part 36 offers are designed to encourage parties to settle disputes without going to court. As mentioned in Bill's case, two offers were made in the proposed settlement of the claim. The choice was: 'take the money and run', as Elton John did (£1,000,000 and an apology) or 'follow the yellow brick road' as Bill Roache did—and go to court. It is a game of brinkmanship for legal counsel and a gamble for the claimant because, as Bill was soon to discover, legal costs escalate very quickly.

Significantly, the court is not made aware of a Part 36 offer until after it has reached a judgment but before it makes an order in relation to the costs of proceedings. In Bill Roache's case, he was coincidently awarded £50,000—the exact same amount as the Part 36 offer made by *The*

Sun. That meant that he was liable for all costs—or about £800,000 when the dust finally settled.

Bill's counsel immediately applied to Mr Justice Waterhouse for their client to be awarded costs and the judge agreed. *The Sun* appealed and one year later the Court of Appeal held that the judge was wrong. This meant that Bill had to pay his own legal bills as well as *The Sun's*—for both the initial case and the appeal. If the jury had awarded him £50,000 and one pound sterling more, together with interest, he would have stood to receive around £85,000. He won the libel case but now owed hundreds of thousands of pounds in legal fees. It was a Pyrrhic victory—a symbolic triumph but an actual defeat. Bankruptcy for Bill Roache soon followed.

This story could end here—in disappointment and acrimony—if it were not for the opportunities for personal growth and responsibility that adversity presented. How did the case and its consequences affect Bill Roache? And what lessons, if any, can be learnt from such experiences? The first lesson was about ego and mindfulness. As he says,

> *At the time I felt I was making a point. If I was successful, then perhaps other people wouldn't have to suffer in the same way. But now I know it was just pride. I think I knew it then, although I didn't want to admit it, not even to myself … instead I defended it and retaliated. If I had just let it ride, people would have forgotten about it in a few days.*

The second lesson for him was to learn that every difficult situation is an opportunity for personal growth.

> *I wasn't even aware I needed the lesson … but you need hard lessons to develop. Difficult experiences are precious gifts. They give you the opportunity to go through the mill. You don't want to, of course, but if you do, you emerge better and stronger as a result.*

> *You shouldn't react, you shouldn't respond, you should just try to understand and forgive. That was the lesson I needed to learn.*

Many years later, on reflection, he was to write in *Life and Soul*,

> *It was a lesson for me—a lesson in pride and a lesson in forgiveness … to see that he [Ken Irwin] was just doing his job and the story would have been forgotten in a week or two. I've had to forgive myself for not taking the opportunity [at Euston Station] … to let it go … and forgive myself for the anger I felt too. It was a hard lesson, and it took years to recover from it financially. But it was my lesson and I accept that. We can't change what has happened to us … but we can change how we respond to it. We can step back from anger and respond with love.*

Significantly, Bill and Sara's response as a couple also involved the very commendable step of taking complete responsibility for their legal debts and working with the bankruptcy trustee to meet their obligations in full. Bill's final word on *William Roache v. News Group Newspapers Ltd, Kelvin MacKenzie (editor) and Ken Irwin (journalist)* is,

> *The court case was a big watershed in my thinking. I had been seeking security in the material world and that wasn't right. Everything is subject to decay and change. The only permanence is your immortal state, your state of being and soul. This is liberating, totally liberating.*

In addition to spiritual growth, what happened after the court's final judgment shows the earthly importance of Bill acknowledging that he was solely responsible for the choices he made, together with an acceptance that he could not blame others for these same choices. Psychologists say that his behaviour demonstrates several essentials: honesty, compassion and respect, fairness, accountability, and courage. This resulted in a willingness to 'clean up his own mess'—the details of which illustrate the inner workings of British libel law. His is a story of our times but, significantly, it says something important and personal about the man himself.

CHAPTER SIX
Politics
'The Flynn Effect'

William 'Bill' Roache and Kenneth 'Ken' Barlow—there is no actor and no fictional character in British popular culture that so perfectly illustrates the two great traditions of modern British liberal parliamentary democracy. Bill Roache, a supporter of the centre-right Conservative Party and Ken Barlow, a social activist aligned with the centre-left of the British Labour Party—in fact, the most famous fictional reader of *The Guardian*, a newspaper that attracts readers of the mainstream left of UK political opinion.

In May 2009, Ken Barlow caused viewer alarm following a scene at the *Coronation Street* newsagent and corner-store the Kabin, when he (as it turned out, temporarily) cancelled subscriptions for both *The Guardian* and *The New Statesman*—another progressive publication often referred to as 'of the left, for the left'. The unfounded concern of some viewers was that Ken Barlow might start buying the right leaning *Daily Telegraph*—a practical illustration of the ideological divide in Britain. So, what defines 'the right' and 'the left' and what does this tell us about Bill and Ken and about our times?[1]

It is said that we define ourselves in terms of our opposites—and on the face of it our politics are no different: the individual and society, morals and ethics, free trade and fair trade, support for employers and support for employees, economic freedom, and personal freedom. Generally, conservatives seek the preservation of shared beliefs that they consider essential to human co-existence. But because politics has become bitter, confrontational, and divisive, it could be argued that the 'conservative mind' is bewildered. Under siege, conservatives see themselves as a rock standing in a hard place, defending what they interpret to be traditional morals and values. This also includes a nod to practical experience (sometimes referred to as common sense or perception) as opposed to empirical knowledge, which is considered by some as 'bookish'—or scientific in nature.

In contrast, progressives define the world based on so-called modern life, with science as their guiding model for knowledge and reason. This tends to elevate the expert to the highest authority while rejecting intuitive points of view. And like conservatives, progressives are also

---

[1] The terms 'left-wing' and 'right-wing' were originally used to identify the physical seating arrangements of politicians during the French Revolution.

confounded by people who do not accept their views—
especially those who reject the so-called best evidence.

The 'progressive mind' on the other hand is especially
alarmed by the conservatives' exercise of moral absolutism,
which they interpret as bigotry and discrimination.
Instead, progressives consider themselves the gatekeepers
of a different set of principles, notably the elimination
of inequalities and injustices. This includes the fair
distribution of state resources and the promotion of
human diversity. This all sounds complex—because it is.[2]
Winston Churchill once described liberal democracy
as, 'an appalling muddle, riddled with faults, dangers,
unfairness, and contradictions', which sounds like most
human beings. In this way, simplistic labels such as 'right'
or conservative and 'left' or progressive neither fully
recognise the human complexities that the esteemed
former Prime Minister observed, nor do they explain the
political choices Bill Roache has made either.

The reality is that most people hold a range of sometimes
contradictory and occasionally changing views that
encompass elements of both orientations. Not all

---

[2] An example of how complex this has become can be found in
the opposing interpretations of the term 'woke' from the African
American vernacular 'stay woke' or showing concern about racism
and social inequality. Opponents of 'being woke' are not in favour
of racism or inequality, but rather are opposed to people who are
opposed to it. In doing so they are, for all intents and purposes, anti
anti-racism and anti anti-inequality. In fact, they say that racism
and the existence of social inequalities are myths, but if they weren't
myths, of course they would be against them.

conservatives conserve everything and not all radicals oppose everything. For instance, research by YouGov, an international data and analytics group headquartered in London, has found that many people are a bit of both Bill and Ken at the same time.

> *While the most distinct views held by left- and right-wing people do fit well with the stereotypical view of left- and right-wing, there are many policy areas where people's views run directly counter to that. For instance, a majority of left-wing Britons (59%) believe that school discipline should be stricter, making it the most commonly held right-wing view among the left. Likewise, 55% of left-wingers believe criminal justice in Britain to be too soft, a plurality of 47% want to see tighter restrictions on immigration, and sizeable minorities of 39% support capital punishment and 36% support Britain having a nuclear arsenal.*
>
> YouGov[3]

According to YouGov Profiles, 28% of Britons describe themselves as left-wing and 25% consider themselves right-wing. A further 19% place themselves in the centre, and the remaining 29% don't know, don't care, are not bothered, or just have other priorities.

YouGov's research, however, shows that for most people, politics—and morality for that matter—is a precarious

---

[3] yougov.co.uk/topics/politics/articles-reports/2019/08/14/left-wing-vs-right-wing-its-complicated

balance of what they approve of and what they dislike. For example, the view that right-wingers are most likely to hold compared to left-wingers is that it was right for Britain to leave the EU, while the view that left-wingers are more likely to hold is that the NHS would be improved by less private sector involvement.[4] In coming to this conclusion, it is as if conservatives tell themselves, 'Here is a rule book that I can accept, which does not impinge on the way I want to live. If only we all followed these rules, everything would be as it should.' For conservatives, questioning the status quo creates unnecessary confusion and conflict. Conversely, progressives are inclined to tell themselves, 'Many of the rules are unjust and should be challenged and changed.'

Significantly, the integrity of Bill and Ken—conservatism and progressivism, right and left, and all shades in between—can only be sustained by the preservation of free thought and expression, and by a personal capacity to exchange views. The alternative is the increasing emergence of extremism. Accordingly, our ideas should be constantly challenged and refined—as Bill Roache has done—in everything from acting to ageing and from politics to spirituality.

Coronation Street was designed to be implicitly political. This was apparent from the very first episode. The subject was class consciousnesses and social mobility. The narrative tension produced by different world views

---

[4] Ted Heath, a conservative, brought the UK into the EU in the first place.

inspired countless future storylines, not least Ken Barlow's celebrated *Survival Magazine* critique of working-class Salford and the seven days he spent in prison after being arrested on an anti-Vietnam War student march. To this end, *Coronation Street* was a recipe with quality ingredients—working-class realism and escapism, job insecurity and money worries, relationships, gossip, football, and the pub—a 'kitchen sink drama', featuring a resilient working-class community characterised by strong women. In clear contrast, out all on his own, was university-educated Ken Barlow, and his great aspirant passions: history, politics, and theatre—and for dramatic effect—a romantic interest in many strong resilient women.

Coronation Street's political roots are hardly surprising. Granada Television's original owner, the notable early anti-fascist Sidney Bernstein (Baron Bernstein) had close pre-war affiliations with the British Communist Party. Sidney Bernstein, who was a co-founder of the London Film Society, understood the power of cultural representations and narratives, having played a major role in the UK Ministry of Information during the Second World War.

There is evidence that Sidney Bernstein, like many of the left at the time, was influenced by the work of Richard Hoggart—the 'father of Cultural Studies', who had a major influence on how his contemporaries viewed working-class life in the North. Hoggard's nostalgic analysis of working-class life clearly influenced early *Coronation*

Street scriptwriters.[5] Sidney Bernstein was later described by the British Film Institute as, 'the dominant influence on the growth and development of commercial television in Britain'. However, as Bill Roache is careful to point out, it was Sidney's younger brother Cecil Bernstein, the founding Chairman of Granada Television, who first championed the idea of *Coronation Street.*

Political representations in *Coronation Street* are sometimes implied but often deliberate. An example of the former can be seen in the special episode, *Farewell Mike*, broadcast on 7 April 2006. In the show, included in *The Best of Coronation Street*, the two rivals—'Barlow the lefty do-gooder' and 'Baldwin, the cut-and-thrust money grabber' reconcile their considerable differences. Mike Baldwin (Johnny Briggs) was a *Corrie* fixture from 1976 to 2006. His time on 'The Street' in fact eclipsed the years of Margaret Thatcher's Prime Ministership (1979 to 1990). And for good reason.

Cockney wide boy Mike Baldwin's character reflected the hard-edge of 1980s neoliberalism, which emphasised deregulation, a flexible labour market, the privatisation of state-owned enterprises and a frontal assault on the power and influence of trade unions—all grist for the character's undergarment mill—and a source of constant ideological angst for poor and painfully principled Ken Barlow.

---

[5] Hoggart defined working-class culture in terms of speech and thought, language and assumptions, social attitudes, and daily practice. This included understanding the moral compass points that reflected on their actions, preferences, and choices.

Although it must be said that Mike Baldwin didn't have a political bone in his body, in contrast to earnest Ken Barlow. On the other hand, Mike Baldwin's ('the king of knickers') great aspirant passions were giving his workers grief, a single malt whisky and a lamb hotpot and for dramatic effect—an appetite for strong resilient women, with bedpost notches almost equal to the great lothario himself, Ken Barlow.

The well-considered (and politically calculated) 1998 story of Deirdre Rachid (Anne Kirkbride) being unjustly jailed for credit card and mortgage fraud inspired a nationwide—and indeed international campaign (*The Irish Times*) to pressure Granada Television to, 'free the Weatherfield *Wan* (One)'. Despite Rachid being a fictional character, notables such as Miss Ireland (Andrea Roche) and politicians from the Labour Prime Minister (Tony Blair) to the leader of the Conservative Opposition (William Hague) to the Home Secretary (Jack Straw) expressed views on the 'injustice'—from both inside and outside Parliament—as if the character had been imprisoned in real life.

Free Deidre posters were plastered on telegraph poles all over Britain. Specially designed T-shirts were printed. Collectable coffee mugs were commissioned. *The Sun* and the *Daily Mirror* even got involved with headlines such as 'We'll Get You Out, Chuck!' and 'Don't Panic … Deirdre Gets Out in 3 Months'. Incredibly, even *The Times*, that long-time stalwart of the Establishment, published a front-page story. And an indignant Ken Barlow provided a character reference and gave evidence in court. (On release from custody in 1999, in fine *Corrie* fashion, the two—Ken and Deirdre—were romantically reunited at a Valentine's disco.)

The British public had become very comfortable with Ken Barlow the stereotypical bleeding-heart, left-leaning-liberal, and so it took some considerable adjustment on the part of fans to accept Bill Roache, the Conservative Party supporter—although this was not a totally unexpected development. Bill Roache, as the son and grandson of medical doctors, describes his family as 'natural Tories'. At one point, his father was even a Conservative Party member of the local Ilkeston Council. As Bill Roache says, 'He was approached … did his bit … and withdrew after one term.' However, at one General Election, Bill Roache remembers that his parents voted for the Labour Party; and they were not alone.

This was the 1945 General Election that brought Clement Attlee to power in a landslide victory. Accordingly, the Britain of Bill Roache's formative years was committed to fundamental social reform. This especially included full employment—an aspiration that was not questioned until the mid-1970s. The importance and role of education in social re-engineering was likewise well understood. The Education Act 1944 raised the school leaving age to 15 and education was free for every child. Many bodies were nationalised, which after the Second World War helped give a job to everyone (especially returned servicemen and women).

To understand Bill Roache's decision to become a public supporter of the Conservative Party, the tumultuous political landscape of post-war Britain needs to be mapped out and explained—and this is very much a story of the times and life of the man. The nationalisation process, for example, began with the Bank of England and civil aviation, followed by the railways and mines. Gas and electricity were then nationalised in 1948. In that same year, the National Health Service came into being—a unique institution, still treasured by most, especially during the Covid-19 pandemic, and widely regarded as the most enlightened piece of British legislation of the 20th century. In 1949, iron and steel were nationalised. By 1950, the state controlled 20% of the economy. This was the way the country was to be run for the next 30 years— the new normal of Bill's formative years.

Britain also became more humane. The Criminal Justice Act 1948 abolished flogging and tried, but failed, to abolish hanging. (The last hangings in the UK were of convicted murderers, Gwynne Evans and Peter Allen, in 1964. The last woman hanged was Ruth Ellis in 1955.) Getting a divorce became slightly easier to obtain. The government made inroads into class privilege by reducing the power of the House of Lords and ending plural voting so that it became one man (or now one person), one vote.

Britain's socialist utopia was, however, very expensive; the money to pay for it all had to be borrowed by a country already in crippling debt from not only the Second World War but the First World War as well. Incredibly, the final instalment on First World War bonds was not settled until March 2015.[6] For a few years, the situation was manageable, as British exports did well in the absence of competition from Germany and Japan, which initially struggled to recover from the War—but when they cleared the rubble away and returned to production with quality goods in the 1950s, Britain's trade position became dire, quickly.

To make matters worse, the US now completely dominated world commerce and the UK was reduced to a second-class power, a fact that even today is hard for many older British people to accept—especially those of Bill Roache's generation who were born at a time when a fifth of the globe was coloured British Empire pink.

Rationing from the Second World War continued. For the first time in 200 years, Britain was not self-sufficient in textiles and had to import them. The pound was devalued, price controls were introduced and there was a wages freeze. In the 1950 General Election, Labour was returned but with a majority of only six seats. Britain was now obliged to support the US in the war between North and South Korea. Fear of the Soviet Union caused defence spending to increase to 14% of national income. The unions struck for higher wages. In 1951, Clement Attlee called an election and, with the help of Bill Roache's parents, the Conservatives under Winston Churchill, were returned with a majority of 17 seats. Apart from

---

[6] The bond was issued in 1932 by Chancellor Neville Chamberlain to reduce the cost of servicing the war debt.

denationalising steel and road transport, the wartime leader left everything pretty much as it was. The welfare state remained intact—but any new socialist initiatives were abandoned.

In 1952, King George VI died and his daughter Elizabeth came to the throne. In 1953, Mount Everest was conquered by a British team led by John Hunt (later Lord Hunt), marking the ascent by Edmund (later Sir Edmund) Hillary and Nepalese Sherpa Tenzing Norgay as the symbolic 'high-water mark' of the British Empire. (News of the expedition's success reached London in time to be released on the morning of Queen Elizabeth II's Coronation on 2 June. (This news had already been conveyed to Chris Briggs, the proprietor of the Pen y Gwryd Hotel, who woke every guest up at 4 am to climb Mount Snowdon in the dark and toast Her Majesty The Queen.)

Wartime rationing ended in 1954. There was a building boom. In 1955, in his 80s and unwell, Winston Churchill resigned and was succeeded by Anthony Eden who had to resign himself in 1957 over the ill-fated Suez Crisis. Pragmatic Harold MacMillan, a bright patrician, took over leadership of the Conservative Party. It was a period of easy credit. Britons bought cars, televisions, washing machines and refrigerators with gay abandon. By unleashing spending, Harold MacMillan was able to say in July 1957 that working people 'never had it so good'. But the good times came at a great financial cost. In 1961, the government had to borrow another £714 million from the International Monetary Fund.

And the government just kept on spending. Added to this, the rapidly fading vestiges of Empire were expensive to maintain—especially keeping troops in Kenya, Borneo, the Persian Gulf and Germany. (As covered in a previous chapter, Bill Roache served in the British Army between 1953 and 1956 in Jamaica, the Middle East and Germany, placing him squarely in the centre of these developments.) Overseas aid to developing countries continued in the hope of trade agreements. (The French did the same thing but were much more successful at it.) Conscription ended, which meant the regular army had to be properly funded. Defence expenditure continued to rise. The Victorian railways were expensive to maintain. New roads had to be built.

In 1953, Britain still had 8.6% of the world's manufacturing production but, by the end of the 1950s, other economies were moving up. Nationalism was sweeping Africa and the Middle East. By the end of the 1960s, most of the colonies had become independent. As Dean Acheson, the American Secretary of State at the time, remarked in 1962, 'Britain has lost an Empire but not yet found a role.' If these were Bill Roache's formative years, then his 20s were dominated by a very different British political culture from that of his childhood.

British governments of all colours were now at the beck and call of the trade unions, which were intent on full employment, higher and higher wages and better working conditions—regardless of the state of the ailing economy. No government could take them on and, if they tried, they were defeated. The Labour Party even depended on the unions for their everyday operational finances. Education was expanded and the welfare state became even more expensive to run. The result was some of the highest rates of personal taxation in the world, which peaked during the 1960s at an extraordinary 91% for the highest income earners.[7]

The British economy was in sharp decline compared to many other countries—between 1950 and 1966, steel production halved as British shipbuilding was overtaken by the Japanese. The iconic UK car industry was now bankrupt. By 1961, wages were rising 50% faster than industrial output. The UK was famously referred to as the 'sick man of Europe'. But apart from some cosmetic changes, nothing was done. In 1961, Harold MacMillan applied to join the European Economic Community but was vetoed by the French President Charles de Gaulle, who thought that Britain was too close to the US.

In the end, Harold MacMillan was not brought down by the failing economy but rather a sex scandal. (Sex scandals were common fare for the 1960s character incarnation of Ken Barlow, who Bill Roache described at the time as 'a sensitive, thinking chauvinist'. Notwithstanding this, Ken's 1961 marriage to Valerie Tatlock (Anne Reid) was watched by a staggering 20 million viewers).

---

[7] Sir Mick Jagger and Keith Richards of the Rolling Stones remain tax exiles, only permitted to spend a short time every year in the UK. Jagger has houses in France and the West Indies and Richards lives in the US.

Profumo resigned and Macmillan followed on health grounds in 1963. 'Events, Dear Boy, Events,' was his famous reply, when asked by a journalist what the biggest problem was for any government. (This was his most memorable quote, except that there is no record of him ever saying it!) Harold MacMillan was replaced by a Scottish peer, Alec Douglas-Home, who lost the 1964 General Election to Labour's Harold Wilson. (Alec Douglas-Home served only one year.) As David Steel said upon his death in 1995, Douglas-Home was 'the last of the gentleman politicians who had no other motivation than public service'.

Harold Wilson, from Huddersfield, may have sounded like a Southerner to Northerners but to Southerners he still sounded like a Yorkshireman. To bolster his 'man of the people' credentials, he smoked a pipe and drank beer while, in private, he smoked cigars and drank spirits. He also carefully created an association with *Coronation Street*. A promotional tour of Australia in 1966 by characters Elsie Tanner (Patricia Phoenix) and Annie and Jack Walker (Doris Speed and Arthur Leslie) was farewelled by Prime Minister Harold Wilson himself and Chancellor of the Exchequer, James Callaghan, for good measure, from the front door of Number 10 Downing Street, in what was a publicity bonanza for all involved.

Harold Wilson was modern, clever, and wily but he overestimated Britain's position in the world, and he inherited an £800 million trade deficit. His remedy was to increase taxation on both capital gains and dividends. This immediately reduced foreign direct investment. So, he borrowed another £2 billion from the US and started spending it on increasing benefits such as abolishing prescription charges. He even tried to reform the trade unions—but failed as his many predecessors had.

Harold Wilson called another election in 1966 and increased his majority. These, incidentally, were the golden years of *Coronation Street*—and the making of Bill Roache. It was the age of free love, *avant-garde* music, and crazy ideas. The Swinging Sixties were in full force and Harold Wilson went with the flow—as did most people, including Bill Roache and especially Ken Barlow. London was transformed from a ruined bomb site into the capital city of the world. The voting age was lowered to 18. Homosexual acts between consenting adults over 21 were decriminalised and abortion liberalised. The Open University was established.

However, by now, immigration had reached a total of 600,000. Social tensions caused by a lack of assimilation were rising—rapidly. The government recognised the problem by passing the Immigration Act 1968, but it did not solve a growing resentment towards newcomers. In 1967, Harold Wilson applied to join the European Economic Community, now a free market of 250 million people, but was again vetoed by Charles de Gaulle who, this time, felt that the UK wasn't close enough to the US.

The government tried to reduce inflation by keeping prices and wages down but, in the following year, a dock strike forced the pound to be devalued, which led to the highest general tax increases since 1939. The public were shocked. By 1970, the economy was showing some small signs of improvement and Harold Wilson took a gamble and called an election.

In the run up, Harold Wilson visited the *Coronation Street* set and even sang a duet with Violet Carson (Ena Sharples) at the Royal Lancaster Hotel in London while presenting the Sun TV Awards. (In their day, Prime Ministers Margaret Thatcher and Tony Blair, and in turn the Labour opposition leader Ed Miliband [who took 'selfies' with the cast], all visited the *Coronation Street* set). Wilson lost to Conservative Edward Heath, an Oxford-educated son of a carpenter and a maid. Labour was punished by receiving the lowest share of the popular vote since 1935.

An example of the subtle incorporation of politics into *Coronation Street* scripts can be seen in an episode broadcast on 4 December 1972. Here Stan and Hilda Ogden (Bernard Youens and Jean Alexander) mention the country's wages being frozen by 'Ted'—a reference to then Prime Minister Edward Heath's announcement of the Counter-Inflation Bill. Edward Heath had hoped to be an innovator. Instead, nationwide industrial strife characterised his tenure, as did The Troubles in Northern Ireland.

Over the next ten years, things went from bad to worse, a situation that was closely reflected in the stark realism of many *Coronation Street* storylines, such as those set in the fictitious Mark Brittain Warehouse, a distribution centre located in Coronation Street from 1971 to 1975. This included industrial action, divided class loyalties and redundancy, with Ken Barlow having a factory floor affair with the attractive union shop steward Peggy Barton (Lois Daine).

In the real world, Edward Heath made the mistake of reversing Labour's financial policy, which was ironically finally working. He reduced taxes and relaxed credit controls. House prices in London doubled between 1971 and 1972. The cost of living in the UK increased by 10% and wages by 18%. Government expenditure was now 52% of national income. There were strikes by the miners and dockers, while the railwaymen worked to rule. Industrial action was banned by the government, but this was ignored. The gas workers and even, horror of horrors, the civil servants, went on strike. Ten million days were lost to strikes in 1970, 13 million in 1971, and 24 million in 1972. Against all their principles, the Conservatives had to save industries by nationalising them, among them Rolls Royce and the Upper Clyde Shipyard.

On top of this, the global economy was rocked and shocked by the 1973 oil embargo by the members of the Organisation of Petroleum Exporting Countries (OPEC). The situation got so bad that Edward Heath introduced a three-day working week just to save energy. On 5 February 1974, the miners voted to go on strike again and Edward Heath called an election—and lost. The country had never been more divided. By March 1974, the price of oil had risen nearly 400% from US$3 a barrel to nearly

US$12. The only good news was that 'black gold' had been discovered in the North Sea. It came online towards the end of the 1970s, a stroke of astonishing good luck for the future Prime Minister, Margaret Thatcher.

In the meantime, things just got worse, and a sizeable proportion of the British people was running out of patience—including Bill Roache. *Coronation Street* storylines of the times saw Ken Barlow frequently discussing politics with characters such as the religious and painfully principled Ernest Bishop (Stephen Hancock) and the perpetually snobby Weatherfield Mayoress, Annie Walker (Doris Speed), who, like Bill Roache, appeared in the very first episode of the show in 1960. Bishop, Walker and Barlow provided 'The Street's' scriptwriters with a safe creative space for discussing otherwise very risky political ideas. Notably, in contrast to the Tory-supporting Annie Walker, Doris Speed was a socialist in the same way as Bill Roache was a conservative playing the socialist Ken Barlow.

Meanwhile, Britain had obligations to the former colonies to allow their citizens to live in Britain. In the late 1950s, Commonwealth immigrants reached 26,000 a year. By the 1960s, it was 100,000 a year. In response, the idea of introducing a non-white family to *Coronation Street* was considered by producers but abandoned because producers were afraid it would upset viewers. It wasn't until 1994 that the show featured its first regular non-white (Asian) family—the Desai clan, who stereotypically took over Fred Elliott's (John Savident) local corner shop. This was quickly followed by *Coronation Street's* first Muslim family, the Nazirs in 2013 followed by 'The Street's' first black family in 2019.[8]

Restrictions were imposed by the Commonwealth Immigration Act 1962 but crippling demands on social services, the creation of ethnic ghettos and increasing social tensions were now well apparent. Nevertheless, in fine island fashion, basic consensus continued to rule, no matter which political party was in power. The traditional, time-honoured system was followed by all until Margaret Thatcher burst upon the national stage in 1979.

This is the context in which, after 23 years of the British public identifying Ken Barlow as a Labour man, Bill Roache declared his very public support for Margaret Thatcher's second term as Prime Minister. It was a bombshell—not least for his local (and controversial) Conservative MP Neil Hamilton (later of UK Independence Party [UKIP] fame) who, like everyone else at the time, just assumed that Bill and Ken were both Bolsheviks.

Many people seemed unable to grasp that Bill was a professional actor playing the part of a totally fictional character. However, once the word was out, the Conservative Party machine kept one of Britain's most famous faces well-occupied—especially with after-dinner speeches at constituency fundraisers. There were even invitations for Bill and Sara Roache to dine at Downing

---

[8] Between 1983 and 1989 Shirley Armitage (Lisa Lewis) played *Coronations Street's* first regular black character.

Street and a reciprocal visit by the new Prime Minister and her husband Denis to the *Coronation Street* set in Manchester, where Bill Roache observed,

> *Even those who weren't of her (Margaret Thatcher's) political persuasion said later how delightful she was.*

As evidence of bipartisan consistency, years later, Bill Roache visited Number 10 again, this time when Tony Blair was Prime Minister. Bill Roache, in typical diplomatic fashion, described the Labour leader as 'having a better sense of humour than Margaret Thatcher'. To Bill's surprise, Cherie Blair, who was aware that it was his birthday, baked him a chocolate cake—herself. Commendable.

Bill Roache may have been in with the Tory establishment but the alliance came at a cost—as it always does. In his autobiography *Ken and Me*, he writes,

> *You live under the impression that everyone loves you but try walking around Bury Market as a representative of the Conservative Party and suddenly you find that there are a lot of people who don't love you. People shout things like, "I'm not going to watch your show anymore," and, "I never thought you were like that."*

For Bill, his decision to publicly support Mrs Thatcher was not an overnight fancy but rather, like many others who drew the same conclusions, his views were substantially formed in the decade leading up to the 1983 General Election. The fact was, by the middle of 1975, inflation was running at 25%. Public expenditure was 60% of national income. Nationalised industries ran up enormous deficits—yet wages increased by 35%. The private sector suffered numerous bankruptcies. The world had lost confidence in Britain and Bill Roache, like many millions of his fellow Britons, had lost confidence in the political status quo.

Labour Prime Minister Harold Wilson, aged 60 and exhausted, resigned in 1976 and handed power over to James Callaghan. Money haemorrhaged from the national economy. The value of the pound plummeted. Unemployment rose sharply. The country was forced to turn again to the International Monetary Fund, this time for a loan of £2.3 billion. (The deal involved the imposition of a strict monetarist policy, especially spending limits, with the guarantee of no further deficit budgets.) Under these circumstances, unemployment had to be accepted as a reality, which was anathema to the unions. James Callaghan only had a parliamentary majority of one seat and was forced to make a pact with the Liberals.

In 1978, the Labour government asked for four years of wage restraint but the unions were having none of it. So, it was back to strikes and more strikes. Automobile workers got 17%. The lorry drivers 25%. Public sector workers then went on strike too. Schools were closed. Rubbish piled up on the streets. Even the dead were left unburied during the 'Winter of Discontent' (1978–79). James Callaghan was at a trade conference in the sunny Caribbean during the worst of it. When he returned to cold damp Albion, looking tanned and fresh-faced, a journalist at the airport asked what he was going to do about the mounting crisis. He replied, 'I don't think that other people in the world share the view that there is a mounting crisis.' The next day *The Sun* screamed the headline, *Crisis, What Crisis?* It was James Callaghan's most famous line and, like Harold MacMillan before him, it was penned by someone else.

The Labour government lost a vote of no confidence in Parliament. An election was called and Margaret Thatcher, Britain's first female Prime Minister, the 'Iron Lady', won with a comfortable and workable 44-seat majority (with plenty of support from *The Sun* and *News of the World*).[9] Margaret Thatcher was a consummate populist, and the country was in for a seismic shift, a political revolution, and a historical turning point as momentous as the Reformation, the Great Depression, or the Second World War. Consensus was dead. Everything was up for grabs and about to change and that included what the *Corrie-*

---

[9] In 1976, a Soviet propaganda outlet known as *Krasnaya Zvezda* (a mouthpiece for the Soviet Army) published an unremarkable article condemning a British politician named Margaret Thatcher who had just taken leadership of the UK Conservative Party, then the opposition party. Robert Evans, then the Reuters bureau chief in Moscow, saw the article and decided to write it up. Evans wrote, 'British Tory leader Margaret Thatcher was today dubbed "the Iron Lady" by the Soviet Defence Ministry.' The phrase immediately caught on in the British press, with Thatcher herself immediately using the term to describe herself.

mad British viewing public thought about Bill Roache and his enthusiasm for 'Thatcher the Milk Snatcher', 'Attila the Hen', and 'The Great She-Elephant'.

Bill provides some insight into his decision to declare his political hand.

> *I felt that it was the time to make my feelings known. Also, I didn't really like the fact that because Ken Barlow was a committed socialist, a lot of people automatically assumed that I was too. I wanted to stand up for my own beliefs.*

Margaret Thatcher, née Roberts, the Oxford educated daughter of a Grantham grocer, represented reward for thrift, hard work and enterprise. And she promised her own brand of radical right-wing reform: to neuter the unions, reduce government spending, cut taxes, and 'release the individual's potential'. The government's sell-off of council housing to private occupiers produced a decisive ideological turning point with a part-rent, part-buy scheme delivering mortgage-free housing to some 200,000 workers in 1982 alone. Inflation fell to 5%. The Falklands War was won. North Sea oil revenues conveniently rose—and kept on rising.

Political and economic power were no longer the sole preserve of aristocrats and the landed gentry, rather Margaret Thatcher's burgeoning middle-class supporters now had a slice of the pie. And it seemed that the proletariat was in on it as well, voluntarily annihilating itself in an orgy of home ownership, kitchen white goods and family holidays on the Costa de Sol. It was into this rich social and political maelstrom that Bill Roache, in his own words, 'came out as a Tory'. In fact, he was just what Mrs Thatcher was looking for—a poster boy for the ascendant middle-class. In one of her famous speeches, it was as if she was talking directly to Bill Roache.

A man's right to work as he will, to spend what he earns, to own property, to have the state as servant and not as master—these are the British inheritance.

If the fictional Mike Baldwin was typical of those who aspired to the crude material benefits of Thatcherism, then the *real* Bill Roache was in many ways a model of what the affluent worker aspired to be—a self-made, successful, self-reliant individual, with social status and a comfortable disposable income, rightly rewarded for his hard work. If this is what the Conservative Party found in Bill Roache, then what Bill Roache found in the Conservative Party was,

A political philosophy that says you are responsible for your actions … with freedom to express yourself—law abiding and financially sound—with compassion towards the less fortunate.

Margaret Thatcher's brand of conservatism was a centre-right rule book that Bill Roache could clearly live with—almost the antithesis of the left-wing political activism so faithfully represented in the character of Ken Barlow and his many memorable storylines. This especially included Ken Barlow's time as the crusading editor and later owner of the fictional free community newspaper, the *Weatherfield Recorder*.

So, what does Bill Roache think of Ken Barlow—and his politics—because the two were, and continue to be, fashioned in the same political and social caldron? How have the political essences of each mixed and matched from the original 'high drama to light-hearted comedy' character created by Tony Warren in 1960? An interesting metaphor is that Ken Barlow's accent has subtly changed over time from a soft Lancashire lilt to the neutral received pronunciation of Bill Roache's own voice.

According to Bill, Ken is 'earnest and honourable' as well as 'stubborn and uncompromising in his political views, a liberal, fair-minded guy always looking to right the wrongs of society', and 'a man of integrity who fights for what he thinks is right'. (Bill has clearly been very careful over the years not to criticise the character too harshly.)

Looking back on it now, I realise that being Ken in the 1960s wasn't just about playing the character, it was also about getting used to what he meant to the public ...

Ken's a well-meaning sort of chap, an ex-teacher who wants to do right by the world and he is always trying to keep the peace in his wonderfully dysfunctional family.

In drawing a distinction between actor and character, Bill Roache has also fundamentally defined *himself*—in terms of his own political opposite. As Bill says,

> *I wasn't like him [Ken Barlow]—I was from a middle-class background and Ken wasn't; I'd have a go at most things, but Ken wouldn't. Fortunately, all I had to do was like him, understand him, believe him, and as I've said, take him through the circumstances that were written for him. And that was fine. That I could do.*

But there were limits to this. In his biography *Ken and Me* Bill Roache continues,

> *What I dislike are people who come up and shout slogans at you: "You've climbed to where you are on the back of the workers," somebody once accused me. I've not climbed on anybody's back. I inherited nothing from my father and became an actor in my own right, and went through a lot of problems, insecurities, and difficulties along the way.*

Intriguingly, while there are clear differences between actor and character, it also appears that in Bill Roache's mind there is a certain similarity between Margaret Thatcher and Ken Barlow, as unlikely that may seem at first blush; one he describes as 'a conviction politician'—the other 'a man of his convictions'. Still, despite his public endorsements, readers of Bill's books can be forgiven for thinking that his support for Mrs Thatcher was not completely unqualified. His public commitment to her seems to have come with caveats. Subtle, sensible cautions pepper his autobiographies.

> *Politicians—men and women—are not infallible. No political party is perfect. It needs to adjust and grow and rectify the inevitable mistakes it will make.*

> *Margaret Thatcher … was well meaning … trying to take the country forward to where it should be, law-abiding and prosperous.*

There was, however, no such apprehension for Margaret Thatcher's successor John Major whom Bill championed as 'Britain's best post-Second World War Prime Minister'. In 1992, he opened John Major's Conservative Party campaign rally in Manchester and created a positive impression with the soon-to-be national leader. A private lunch at Chequers, the Prime Minister's country residence in the village of Ellesborough, Buckinghamshire, soon followed with the two men establishing a friendship that lasts to this day. (And like many people, Sir John Major's wife, the philanthropist Dame Norma Christina Elizabeth, Lady Major—was and by all reports continues to be a *Corrie* fan.)

Interestingly, Bill Roache supported Leave in the 2016 Brexit referendum in which 52% voted to leave and 48% voted to remain in the EU, (although his position was very low key—not surprising given the acrimony that characterised the public debate). The result was

17,419,742 voted to leave, 16,141,241 to remain with a staggering 31,048,080 either not registering or not voting. In contrast to Bill Roache, John Major broke ranks on Brexit with many of his conservative colleagues (joining David Cameron and Theresa May). Yet he and Bill remain friends. And this is where it gets interesting. As Bill says,

> *That doesn't mean I think everything the Conservative Party does is right. I can be as critical as anyone when it goes wrong and when it makes the wrong decisions. One isn't blinded by slavish dogma.*
>
> *One of the great things about democracy and this country is our capacity to agree to disagree. In other countries, opposition to the status quo can land you in prison or in front of a firing-squad, and revolutions are held in place of elections …. We should value and respect the democracy we have, and the freedom of speech it allows.*
>
> *I respect opposing points of view and am always ready to listen and discuss them with people.*

Bill's words are a timely reminder of the importance of unlearning the now fashionable idea that we hate each other just because we disagree on something. His experience presents the possibility that history can be more than 'a victory of the heartless over the mindless' (to quote *Yes Minister's* Sir Humphrey Appleby) and that changing your mind about something actually shows that you have a mind.

Bill's accommodating position is a strong case for the view that to understand someone you must avoid superficial assumptions and oversimplifications—especially against the backdrop of Bill and Ken, the two sides of the coin, as it were, of British political culture. And this is also an opportunity to go beyond viewing Bill Roache through a narrow strictly bipartisan lens, to rather discover a man of conviction who established his own political identity in the face of significant public disquiet—and refused to be held captive to ideological dogmas. Indeed, in the life of the man, we see both thoughtful conservatism and a well-considered questioning of the status quo. We see both 'right' and 'left'. And after 60 years of *Coronation Street* in 2021, Bill has grown and adapted to celebrate Ken's differentness as more than a character he plays. Rather, as Bill now says, 'Ken is another being, like a close friend that I inhabit and work with. Very few people have ever done that.'

It is at this point that Bill seems to leave the world of politics and, like many people, he just moved on with his life. He says that, as a young man, he had no interest in politics and while he has been, 'approached on a couple of occasions to run for public office' he has strongly rejected the advances. And now, as an older man, and especially since the publication of *Life and Soul*, politics seems to have become irrelevant to him again—rather his priorities are,

To look for agreement and not conflict, discuss rather than argue, laugh, love and keep things

simple, meditate, and be a good listener—and most of all look after the present.

As the YouGov research shows, not taking an interest in politics is an increasingly common position for many people in the UK—Bill included. Indeed, in an example of what is called 'the Flynn Effect,' nearly 30% of Britons appear to be joining Bill Roache in concentrating on more ethereal interests.[10]

---

[10] 'The Flynn Effect' theorises that too much involvement in politics is not only ultimately disappointing, but futile.

First XV rugby team, Rydal Senior School, Colwyn Bay, Wales, 1946. (Bill Roache is in the second row fourth from the left.) (Copyright Rydal Penrhos School, reproduced with permission.)

Second-Lieutenant W.P Roache, Royal Welch Fusiliers, 1952. (Copyright private collection of William Roache, reproduced with permission.)

Captain Roache with a group of trainees for the Trucial Oman Scouts, Al Sharjah, 1955. (Copyright private collection of William Roache, reproduced with permission.)

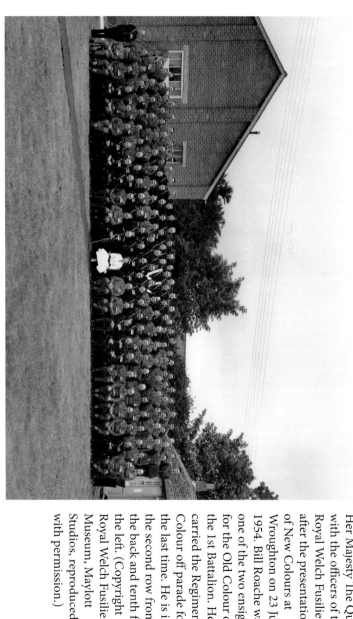

Her Majesty The Queen with the officers of the Royal Welch Fusiliers after the presentation of New Colours at Wroughton on 23 July 1954. Bill Roache was one of the two ensigns for the Old Colour of the 1st Battalion. He carried the Regimental Colour off parade for the last time. He is in the second row from the back and tenth from the left. (Copyright Royal Welch Fusiliers Museum, Maylott Studios, reproduced with permission.)

Frank Barlow (Frank Pemberton) with Ken Barlow (Bill Roache) in a scene from the first episode of *Coronation Street*, 9 December 1960. (Copyright ITV, reproduced with permission.)

Bill Roache and Sara McEwan Mottram announce their engagement, 1976. (Copyright private collection of William Roache, reproduced with permission.)

Violet Carson (Ena Sharples), Bill Roache (Ken Barlow), Doris Speed (Annie Walker) and Jack Howarth (Albert Tatlock), 1978. (Copyright ITV, reproduced with permission.)

Jean Alexander (Hilda Ogden), Bernard Youens (Stan Ogden) and Bill Roache (Ken Barlow), 1984. (Copyright ITV, reproduced with permission.)

Sara McEwan Mottram and Bill Roache on their wedding day, 1978. (Copyright private collection of William Roache, reproduced with permission.)

In the Roache family home with Will, Bill, Verity and Sara Roache looking after the litter of nine puppies produced by their labrador, Ella, 1989. (Copyright private collection of William Roache, reproduced with permission.)

Bill Roache with Prime Minister Margaret Thatcher visiting the set of *Coronation Street*, 1990. (Copyright ITV, reproduced with permission.)

Bill Roache (Ken Barlow) welcoming His Royal Highness Prince Charles to the *Coronation Street* set together with cast members (right to left) Simon Gregson (Steve McDonald), Jennifer James (Geena Gregory), and Tina O'Brien (Sarah Platt), 2000. (Copyright ITV, reproduced with permission.)

Bill Roache meeting Her Majesty The Queen during her visit to Preston, Lancashire, 2002. (Copyright private collection of William Roache, reproduced with permission.)

Bill Roache welcoming Her Majesty The Queen to the *Coronation Street* set July 2021, to mark the show's 60th anniversary. With (from left to right) Barbara Knox (Rita Tanner) Sue Nicholls (Audrey Roberts) and Helen Worth (Gail Platt.) Copyright ITV reproduced with permission.)

CHAPTER SEVEN
Acting
Mighty Oaks from Little Acorns Grow[1]

Scriptwriters create characters in their imaginations and actors bring them to life through committed and convincing characterisations. In doing so, audiences discover that acting is no less than the refinement of our ability to communicate with each other—authentically. These transactions commence as soon as we are born, as each of us, in our own way, develops a sort of internal theatre that enables us to abandon our apprehensions and join the communion of others. A skilled actor like Bill Roache will do this.

For actors, their craft weaves all the gestural and spoken elements of the human body together to produce the suspension of disbelief in their audience. An accomplished actor will enthral to such a degree that belief becomes

---

[1] From a 14th century English proverb meaning great things come from small beginnings.

practically blind to reality, as it has with the character of Ken Barlow. Audiences, however, are not bodies of passive people. Far from it. We really do love being fooled, especially when we know it, and especially when we have paid for the privilege.

Why then is so much creative output concerned with the process of creative output? Why are there so many Hollywood movies about Hollywood? Do creatives want you to know that you are being fooled? Of course, they do. And why? Because the better they fool you, the better they can demonstrate their craft, how hard they work and how deep they dig, both into their skillsets as well as into their life experiences. To quote Marty DiBergi from the rockumentary *This is Spinal Tap* (1984), 'But hey, enough of [our] yakkin; whaddaya say? Let's boogie!'[2]

So, what does Bill Roache himself say and how does this compare across what is essentially three generations of the one family of actors (given the age difference between Linus and James Roache).

> *My definition of acting? Acting is usually considered to be pretending, living in a world of 'make believe'. To me it is the opposite; it is the truth—the truth of the writer—the truth of the character—and the truth of the situation—being in the here and now. It is all about being true.*

[2] In 2002, *This Is Spinal Tap* was declared 'culturally, historically, or aesthetically significant' by the Library of Congress. The movie's improvised dialogue style of storytelling has influenced over three decades of film making from *Borat* to *Curb your Enthusiasm*.

And Bill's eldest son Linus Roache?

For me, acting is about sharing the human experience, and at its height, it's about opening a window to the soul. After all the preparation, research and rehearsal, the challenge is letting go to simply be in the moment. Then ideally, the actor can share without fear or judgment all the beauty and joy as well as the pain and suffering of our common human condition. That's what I aspire to anyway, as lofty as it sounds. And that's what keeps me in love with the art.

And as for Bill's youngest son, James Roache, his equally insightful definition demonstrates that if you ask 100 actors the same question you may get 100 different responses—each sharing many of the same critical threads: authenticity, the abandonment of self, and courage.

Acting is the physicalised embodiment of storytelling. A powerful and emotive medium to empathetically inform, inspire, move, and teach. A noble and courageous profession that requires the performer to surrender any guarded or contrived notions of the self and courageously embrace vulnerability in the presence of spectators.

*****

It was at Michael House Steiner School that Bill Roache first appeared on stage. The school put on what he describes as, 'the Steiner equivalent of nativity plays', and he featured in one as an oak tree. (According to the actor Sally Dynevor, 'oaks are known to live for over 1,000 years and, as such, are a symbol of longevity—a harbinger of Bill's long and successful career as an actor').[3] It was a non-speaking role where he had to stand in the background with his arms outstretched. To steady himself, Bill grabbed hold of the curtains which promptly collapsed on top of him— literally bringing the house down.

But there was another sign, in a world according to Bill Roache in which there is no such thing as a coincidence. The senior boy at Rydal, who first showed him around, was none other than John Howarth, whose father, Jack Howarth, was later to play Valerie Barlow's (Anne Reid) Uncle Albert Tatlock 20 years later—in an extraordinary 1305 episodes of *Coronation Street*.[4]

*****

One day at Rydal, Bill Roache noticed a small group of junior and middle school boys 'lounging about on benches

---

[3] In the ancient forests of Britain, oak trees were revered by the Celtic Druids because of their enormous height. It was believed that the top branches reached to heaven while the roots breached the underworld. The Bowthorpe Oak in Manthorpe near Bourne, Lincolnshire, for example, is believed to be England's oldest oak tree with an estimated age of over 1,000 years. The Major Oak in Sherwood Forest Nottinghamshire is a relative youngster at just under 1,000 years old.
[4] The character became such an institution that, in the 1960s grumpy old men were sometimes nicknamed 'Albert Tatlock'. Like Bill Roache, Jack Howarth was also an original *Coronation Street* cast member.

in the school hall'. It was the remnants of the school's dramatic society, which he and his friend Anthony 'Dick' Tuckey, immediately joined. Together they went on to become the school's leading lights, acting together in a half-term production of *Macbeth,* when Dick played the lead role and Bill played Lady Macbeth.[5]

In 1950, the two featured in the school production of *The Miser* by Molière. A contemporary review in *A Dramatic Story: A History of Theatre at Rydal Penrhos School* makes a very favourable mention of Bill's performance.[6]

> *Next to Tuckey's, the most impressive performance was by Roache, in the difficult role of Valère. Here was dignity without woodenness, and an intelligent and faithful understanding which kept the play going in its more static moments.*

At the time, Bill's mother was directing productions for the Ilkeston Women's Guild and she established in her young son the concept of the Deming Cycle or the idea

---

[5] Anthony 'Dick' Tuckey was to go on to Bristol Old Vic Drama School and enjoyed a successful career as artistic director of the Belgrade at Coventry and the Liverpool Playhouse.

[6] The expression, 'The apple doesn't fall far from the tree' has special currency here. In the Rydal 1981 production of Arthur Miller's *The Crucible,* Linus Roache also received a glowing review. 'Proctor himself was as powerful as he has been anywhere. Linus Roache produced a riveting performance building up to an apocalyptic climax. There can be no doubt that Linus is one of the best schoolboy actors seen to date by this writer. His control and his professional approach augur well for a successful career on the stage.'

of continuous improvement: plan, do, check, revise, study and act.[7]

> *But after seeing plays I was in, instead of the usual proud parents 'well done', my mother would hand me notes on how to improve my performance. This was very valuable, and I am sure it contributed to my winning the school drama cup when I appeared in Henrik Ibsen's play,* An Enemy of the People.

Another thing that Bill has Rydal School to thank for was his passion for cinema, which was part and parcel of the school's revised curriculum emphasis on aesthetics. He describes how every Saturday night during winter term, a film would be shown in the school hall, mostly consisting of movies made in the 1930s: Abbott and Costello, Laurel and Hardy, Will Hay, early Hitchcock as well as *The Scarlet Pimpernel* (1934) and *Pygmalion* (1938) both starring the great Leslie Howard.

However, the film that was to influence the young Bill Roache most was *The Jolson Story* (1946) starring Larry Parks. As he says,

---

[7] American Walter Andrew Shewhart (1891–1967) is widely considered the father of 'quality control', which in turn influenced fellow American William Edwards Deming (1900–1993), who is acknowledged as the inventor of Continuous Quality Improvement. Both men's methods were instrumental in Japan's manufacturing recovery after the Second World War. Their paradigm has been applied to everything from health care to acting.

The story of this born showman, a man who could entertain and knew it, who broke with his family background and overcame obstacles to achieve his aims hit a pulse with me. It harmonised totally with whatever it was that made me want to become an actor.

At this point, the question arises about 'nature or nurture' and so the matter of whether great actors are born or made—or both—in what is effectively, a collision of character and circumstance. For example, during his selection course for officer cadet training, Bill was required to prepare a debate on a topic of his choosing. One topic instantly came to mind almost as if it were a seed planted in his brain that only needed nourishment to germinate. As he says,

I picked acting as my theme, not that I knew a great deal about it at that stage, but I assumed the Selection Board wouldn't either. It paid off. Acting didn't really lend itself to hostile cross-examination (and I got away with it).

*****

And then four years passed. Bill Roache found himself out of the army and away from the sun-scorched tranquillity of the Rub' al Khali Desert, living in a cold bedsit in Earl's Court, London, on his own, without friends, and again contemplating his future. Years later, a parent wrote to him saying their daughter 'thinks she wants to be an actor',

'What advice could he give her?' His reply was, 'Wanting to be an actor has nothing to do with it. You are either an actor or you are not. And once you discover that you are, then almost nothing will stop you.' In a case of practising what you preach, Bill says of his own experience,

> *The desire to act, particularly in films, grew stronger and stronger. I used to go to the cinema a lot and, after every film, I'd write down the name of the director and the production company from the end credits. When I got back to the bedsit, I would send a letter asking for work. I must have written hundreds of these letters.*

And, then one day, he received a telegram from Brian Desmond Hurst, at the time widely regarded as Northern Ireland's finest film director, and best known for his 1951 adaptation of Charles Dickens's *A Christmas Carol*. At their first meeting in Belgravia, Hurst immediately propositioned him; the dreaded 'casting couch'. According to Bill, Hurst said, 'I'd like to go to bed with you. But don't worry, I never force myself on anyone.' A shocked look on Bill Roache's face was quickly followed by, 'Right, you have the part. We pay £40 a day, will that be all right?' According to Bill, the answer was 'yes' to the £40, and that was that—'as long as you weren't the last to leave one of Mr Hurst's parties'.

The film was *Behind the Mask*, based on a John 'Jack' Hunter screenplay starring Michael Redgrave (later Sir Michael Redgrave), with Tony Britton, Ian Bannen and

Lionel Jefferies.[8] Vanessa Redgrave (Michael Redgrave's daughter) had one line (it was her first film role too)—and Bill had two lines. As he says,

It was my first acting job. I had seen professional actors at work and gained some insight into how a studio functioned. I was extremely grateful to Brian Desmond Hurst for giving me my first break, but I later found that you never mentioned you had made a film for him because it was automatically assumed you had got the role for the wrong reasons.

Bill Roache's determination was beginning to pay off. He soon received another letter, this time from an executive producer at Beaconsfield Studios, Peter Rogers, who shortly afterwards began producing the iconic *Carry On* films. Bill was offered a small part in the black and white television series *Ivanhoe*, starring Roger Moore[9], in his first major role as Sir Wilfred of *Ivanhoe*.[10] Bill's lines were, 'My Lord, a Knight is coming, and he rides alone! Dismount, Sir Knight! And keep to the path!' It was the only episode of *Ivanhoe* that he ever spoke in—but

---

[8] Jack Hunter was the lover of Soviet Spy Guy Francis de Moncy Burgess while both were students at Cambridge University. Hunter later claimed to be the illegitimate son of Douglas Fairbanks, the actor.

[9] Brian Desmond Hurst also gave Roger Moore his first film role in *Caesar and Cleopatra* (1945) playing a Roman soldier and then helped pay for Roger Moore to attend the Royal Academy of Dramatic Arts.

[10] *Ivanhoe* was shown on ITV between 1958–59. It was aimed at a children's audience with the characters drawn from Sir Walter Scott's novel *Ivanhoe* (1819).

it was not the only episode he appeared in. Whenever the director needed a stock scene with a sentry standing in silhouette on a castle battlement, in a knitted string outfit, a wool balaclava painted silver to look like armour, a prop longbow and a quiver of faux arrows—it was Bill Roache.

And then another reply. A small part in *The Queen's Guards* (released in 1961) directed by Michael Powell, who later described the work as 'the most inept piece of filmmaking that I have ever produced or directed'. Contemporary reviews were 'not kind' (industry code for bloody awful) and the movie practically disappeared after its initial release.

Bill Roache's scene was set in a tent in the desert, and he played a British Army wireless operator (also appearing in several background scenes). Again, there were intriguing parallels between the life experiences of the actor and the storylines of the character. Reflecting Bill's practical approach to the craft of acting, he purposefully stayed on after his modest scenes were shot to observe the dynamic of a film set—and learn.

I was beginning to gain an insight into the art of acting by this time. I realised that if I were lucky enough to have a big opportunity come my way, I wouldn't have the skill and experience to fully exploit it. It is one thing to have an opportunity, quite another to use it in a way that takes you forward. It seemed to me the best place to learn the basic craft

of acting was in the theatre before a live audience.
So, I started to write to theatrical companies.

This resulted in an audition, reading together with the late great actor Albert Finney (who got the part) for the West End production of *Billy Liar*.[11] But more significant were the private acting lessons Bill Roache received at the time from Ellen Pollock, a prolific stage actor, devotee of Bernard Shaw, and longtime president of the Shaw Society.[12] She also tutored him in audition technique and stagecraft.

Bill was beginning to discover the path he needed to follow to advance his career, generally accepted at the time (and still largely acknowledged today—with the addition of drama school) as: a grounding in school theatre, professional acting classes, auditioning, actual experience in front of an audience, a résumé, and an enthusiastic theatrical agent. And so, Bill started to write to agents as well. (The Royal Mail must have done very well out of him because this was before the days of emails, faxes, and texts.)

One of the leading theatrical agents of the day was St James Management, run by Sir Laurence Olivier (later Baron Olivier). Bill wrote to him as well—and incredibly

---

[11] Albert Finney's last role was as Kincade, the caretaker of Skyfall mansion and the Bond family estate gamekeeper, in *Skyfall* (2012).
[12] Most female thespians now refer to themselves as actors, not actresses. The term 'actress' is now mostly reserved for the name of an award, for example, 'The Oscar for best actress goes to …'

got a reply suggesting that the two should meet at the stage door of the Cambridge Theatre where Olivier was appearing in *The Entertainer*, a three-act play by John Osborne.[13] As Bill recounts,

At 7.15 pm, he suddenly strode around the corner and straight up to me. "Mr Roache?" he said. "Do come in." I followed him to his dressing room. He gave me a gin and tonic and offered me a cigarette—an 'Olivier' naturally—and said, "I hope you don't mind me getting ready while we're talking." Then he proceeded to put on his makeup and sort out his wardrobe.

During our talk, the door opened, and that wonderful old actor George Ralph looked in. "This is Mr Roache," Sir Laurence said, introducing me as though I was a colleague or of equal standing. That made me feel absolutely fabulous. Here I was, sitting in the dressing room of the country's most celebrated living actor, and he put me totally at ease.

Eventually Sir Laurence said, "What can I do for you?" "Well, I have come into acting rather late," I explained. I was 25 at the time. "Most of the other actors I've spoken to say I should get out and find a more secure profession. I just thought a word of advice from you would be worth a 100 from anybody else. He said, "Don't give up, that's all I can

---

[13] Contemporary reviews of John Osborne's play *Look Back in Anger* (1956) noted that it had transformed English theatre.

tell you. I had two years myself that were terrible, with nothing happening at all. It was dreadful. But if it's in you, keep at it."

Bill was to later say that this advice inspired him because, 'Hope in its greatest and grandest sense illuminates the way.' Clearly, the meeting with Olivier had a profound influence on him, especially in his exhortation to 'never give up', because others, like the American actor William Redfield, found Olivier to be defined by the same quality.

Laurence Olivier is less gifted than Marlon Brando. He is even less gifted than Richard Burton, Paul Scofield, Ralph Richardson, and John Gielgud. But he is still the definitive actor of the twentieth century. Why? Because he wanted to be. His achievements are due to dedication, scholarship, practice, determination, and courage. He is the bravest actor of our time.[14]

There is a wonderful sequel to this story. Many years later, Bill was making a telephone call in the hallway of the Granada Studios when someone behind him said, 'Hello, I'd just like to say how much I enjoy you on *Coronation Street.*' It was none other than Sir Laurence Olivier.

The next step in Bill's career was to engage the London-based agent Daphne Scorer, who introduced him to a

---

[14] William Aubrey Darlington, (1968) *Laurence Olivier*, Morgan Grampian Books, London. W.A. Darlington was the drama critic at the time for the *Daily Telegraph.*

producer named Norris Staton who, in turn, contracted him for small parts in a summer season for the Unicorn Players, Clacton Town Hall, Clacton-on-Sea.[15] His first play was *The Last Mrs Murdoch*, which he describes as a 'terrible thriller'. After a slow start, the director Donald Masters said of Bill, 'I've never seen anyone improve so much.'

And then another letter arrived, a response from Nottingham Repertory, offering Bill a job as a humble Assistant Stage Manager (ASM). The pay was £6/10 week (about £120 in today's terms and pretty miserable really). There, he joined two other fresh-faced ASMs—one of whom was Brian Blessed. Years later, Blessed incorporated the story of how he and Bill first met into his well-reviewed production, *An Evening with Brian Blessed*, at the Floral Pavilion, New Brighton, on the Wirral Peninsula (2018).

The first of many productions for Bill at Nottingham Repertory was *Hamlet*, in which he took several minor parts with the now veteran Canadian actor Donald Sutherland playing Fortinbras.[16] What followed was a well-reviewed production of *Peer Gynt*, a five-act play in verse by Norwegian dramatist Henrik Ibsen. Bill played five parts with lots of quick changes.

---

[15] Daphne Scorer was also an actor who was active in the 1930s and appeared in *The Good Companions* (1933), *Sunshine Susie* (1931) and *She was only a Village Maiden* (1933).

[16] Fortinbras, the Norwegian Prince, serves as the most important foil for Hamlet. He provides the audience with comparative actions and emotions that in turn better reveal Hamlet's own character.

And still he persisted with his frenetic letter writing campaign, obviously taking Olivier's advice to heart.[17] One letter attracted an invitation from Oldham Repertory Theatre Club (1952–1969) to audition. Oldham was considered by actors at the time to be 'lucky' and for Bill Roache that was certainly to be the case. His now good friend Brian Blessed, who had been to Bristol Old Vic Theatre School, helped him choose the audition piece from *Cat on a Hot Tin Roof* and then coached him.[18] What Bill learned from the experience of working with someone he trusted was,

> *Acting is an ensemble thing. It's like music—the words must flow in harmony and the timing is vital. You get some actors who are very selfish. They will tread on your lines, deliberately cut in, upstage you and generally be uncooperative. You don't discover anything about that sort of thing until you are operating. So, often it is better to have people you know you can trust because you've already worked with them.*

This deep trust obviously exists between Bill and his longtime manager John Hayes, the CEO of Champions

---

[17] In a world where emails can easily be 'trashed' without even being read or considered, an actual letter, with an actual stamp on it, is so novel these days that no one it seems can resist opening and reading it. And if you really want to make an impact, send it first class or priority paid and registered so that the recipient must sign for it.

[18] Written by Tennessee Williams, the three-act play is an adaptation of his short story *Three Players of a Summer Game* (1952), reputed to be his personal favourite. The play won the Pulitzer Prize for Drama in 1955.

UK plc, whom he describes as 'his dearest friend and most trusted confidant'.

In his first week at Oldham Repertory, Bill Roache appeared in a minor role in the popular *Tea and Sympathy*. Written in 1953, it is a play in three acts by Robert Anderson about the character Tom Lee, a student in a New England preparatory school, accused of being a homosexual. The play was first performed in London at the Comedy Theatre, now the Harold Pinter Theatre, under 'membership conditions', because the Lord Chamberlain had imposed an outright ban, a sign of how much things have changed.[19] He was also in a production of *Goodbye, Mr Chips* at Oldham with Alan Rothwell, who later played David Barlow, Ken Barlow's brother in *Coronation Street*.

A play called *Death and Brown Windsor* followed, which Bill described as, 'Like a bad Agatha Christie. It was an awful play. It was all plot, times, dates and red herrings and dreadful to learn.' Bill was on stage with a young Henry Livings, later a prolific playwright and screenwriter, who worked extensively in British television and theatre from the 1960s to the late 1990s.[20]

---

[19] The Lord Chamberlain of the Household is the most senior officer of the Royal Household. For over 230 years, the Lord Chamberlain had the power to decide which plays would be granted a licence for performance. From 1737 to 1968, this meant that the Lord Chamberlain had the capacity to censor theatre at his pleasure. And did.

[20] Henry Livings also appeared as Wilf Haddon, Martha Longhurst's (Lynne Carol) son-in-law, on *Coronation Street* in May 1964.

In the opening scene, the two found themselves going straight to the end of the play. The prompter was called on stage and admitted to losing his place in the script as well. The audience all fell about laughing. Bill later said, 'It's always a good sign because it means that the audience is with you.' *Meet me at Moonlight* (a Victorian musical) and the Oldham Repertory Christmas pantomime *Robin Hood* followed, with Bill cast as the principal boy, complete with a Lincoln green jacket, tights, boots, and a raked felt hat topped with a pheasant feather.

In 1958, while he was still at Oldham, Granada Television was established. Yet another letter was sent, this time to the casting director there. A month, a reply, and an audition later, Bill won small parts in *Skyport,*[21] *Knight Errant,*[22] *Biggles,*[23] the *Bulldog Breed,*[24] and the comedy film *His and Hers*[25]—a roll call of British comedy greats starring Terry Thomas and Kenneth Williams. Then came a 'big break' as the lead role in the prestigious London-based ITV Play of the Week, *Marking Time.* As Bill says in reflection,

---

[21] As airlines were beginning to introduce regular transcontinental services ITV launched *Skyport*, a drama series about the activities at an international airport. Bill Roache's role was uncredited.

[22] Two of *Knight Errant* scriptwriters (Philip Levene and Roger Marshall) later contributed scripts to *The Avengers*. Honor Blackman, who starred as the leather-clad Cathy Gale in *The Avengers*, got some early experience as a guest star. Bill Roache appeared in two episodes, *The Star of Java* (1960) and *Eve and the Serpent* (1960), as the character David Towers, a 'student type'.

[23] Bill Roache's role was uncredited.

[24] Bill Roache played the part of a 'space centre operator'.

[25] Bill Roache played the part of a 'second reporter'.

Looking back on those early attempts to be an actor, I am reminded of someone once asking me, "What particular ability was it that made you want to become an actor?" And I said, it wasn't an ability, it was an inability. A shyness—overcoming shyness. I think this is true for many actors. When you are in television and films, of course, you don't get the feedback from the audience and a lot of actors will finish a scene and turn and say, "Was that all right?" They just want the director to say, "Well done." At some level we're all insecure and seeking approval.

At the end of 12 hectic months at Oldham, performing a play every evening, rehearsing during the day, and learning lines at night, Bill felt that he had been to the best drama school in the world and had more than served his 'apprenticeship'. He was now ready for anything.

There then followed a sequence of events that changed Bill's life—and ultimately British television as well. His agent received a call to say that Granada wanted to talk to him about a series they were planning to do. Initially, he was preoccupied with the imminent release of *Marking Time*. His agent's advice was, 'You might as well go along for the interview, because there is nothing else on—at the moment.' Ironically, Bill was completely relaxed with the casting director, mostly because he wasn't bothered about getting the part. It was not only perfect serendipity but, according to Bill, a sort of 'secret weapon' that aspiring actors can apply to calm their nerves. The show was called *Florizel Street*.

The question of why the original title was changed from *Florizel Street* to *Coronation Street* has been the subject of much speculation. Ken Irwin in his book *The Real Coronation Street* (1970) wrote,

> *It did not remain* Florizel Street, *of course. How could it? Especially after Agnes, the tea lady at Granada, had taken Tony Warren aside one day and said quite calmly and sensibly, "It will never work, y'know, Tony. Not with a name like that. It sounds more like a disinfectant."*

Sean Egan, in his well-researched history of the programme, *50 Years of Coronation Street: The (Very) Unofficial Story* (2010), confirms Ken Irwin's account but adds that Bill Roache had a role to play as well. Bill put the record straight once and for all by confirming, 'A big groan went up as I mispronounced the name in a dry run, and they decided then and there to change it.'

Years later, Bill appeared on the television show *Good Morning* together with *Coronation Street's* creator Tony Warren, who revealed for the first time how Bill landed the role. According to Bill,

> *As a character, Ken was a problem; an intellectual lad from a working-class street who was the first member of his family to attend university. I often wondered if the character was loosely based on Tony himself. Apparently, while I was recording* Marking Time *at Granada, Tony saw me. He*

fetched the casting director, José Scott, pointed me out, and said, "That is Ken Barlow." Obviously, I had to have the initial interview and do the pilot but Tony said that was the moment they gelled it. So, I owe a lot to Tony Warren, as does the rest of the cast, Granada, and I venture to say, the nation.

Significantly, many others owe a debt to *Coronation Street*. As Bill says,

Now that repertory theatre is all but dead, series like Coronation Street have taken its place as seedbeds for new talent. Not just for actors, but writers, producers, directors, and the whole panoply of creative people needed to keep a top-rated show on the screen.

This includes, amongst many, many others, Davy Jones of The Monkeys fame,[26] Peter Noone or 'Herman' of the successful 1960s pop group Herman's Hermits,[27] Sue Johnson,[28] Dame Joanna Lumley (who was already a well-

---

[26] David 'Davy' Thomas Jones's television acting debut was for one *Coronation Street* episode in 1961 as Colin Lomax, the grandson of Ena Sharples.

[27] Peter Blair Denis Bernard Noone played the nephew of Len Fairclough, Stanley Fairclough, in a solo appearance of *Coronation Street* in 1961.

[28] Sue Johnston made her television debut in 1982 with a minor recurring role on *Coronation Street* playing the role of Mrs. Chadwick.

established actor),[29] Tracy Brabin,[30] and Bill's eldest son Linus Roache.[31]

Bill's late wife Sara also first appeared uncredited in *Coronation Street* (on 14 November 1977) playing the role of a receptionist. In the 1980s, Sara Roache's acting career was again blossoming with roles in *Emmerdale, Juliet Bravo* and *Cracker,* as well as an appearance in *Coronation Street* playing the character Judge Alderman.

The journey from the Rydal Drama Society to *Coronation Street* and beyond has effectively made Bill Roache an alumnus of the acting 'school of hard knocks', culminating what he called the 'punishing' experience of repertory theatre—first Nottingham and then Oldman—followed by productions at Hampstead Theatre, Richard Gordon's *Doctor in Love* at the Bradford's Alhambra Theatre, John Bowen's *Disorderly Women* in London and Manchester, and then work on Noël Coward's *Blithe Spirit* and André Roussin's *The Little Hut*, Margaret Williams and Hugh Steadman Williams *Flip Side*, and Alan Ayckbourn's *Time and Time Again* with his own theatre companies, The

---

[29] Dame Joanna Lumley played the role of Elaine Perkins in *Coronation Street* between July and August 1973.

[30] Tracy Brabin is a British Labour and Co-operative politician who has served as the first Mayor of West Yorkshire since 2021. She was the Member of Parliament for Batley and Spen from 2016 to 2021. She played Tricia Armstrong in *Coronation Street* (1994-1997).

[31] Linus Roache played Ken Barlow's eldest son Peter Barlow from 1973-1975. He is best known for playing Robert F. Kennedy in *RFK* (2002) as well as Michael Cutter in *Law and Order* (2008–2010) and *Law and Order Special Victims Unit* (2011–2012) and more recently as Ecgberht King of Wessex, in *Vikings* from 2014-2017.

Stables and William Roache Productions, at the Guildhall Preston.

In contrast, Bill's eldest child has followed what he regards as 'a better path'. Linus Roache has had a classical foundation in acting, the sort of preparation Bill would have wished for himself.[32] This includes Central School of Speech and Drama University of London (where Linus Roache's mother, the celebrated actor Anna Cropper trained) and then 15 years at the Royal Shakespeare Company (Stratford) and the National Theatre.[33] As Bill says, 'He's done it in the way I would have liked but I started late. I had no connections. I had to sort of scramble my way in.'

In reflecting on his extraordinary career in acting, which Bill modestly calls 'an apprenticeship', he makes the following salient comment.

Although the theatre is essential for learning the craft of acting, and a live audience is stimulating and exciting, I have no desire to go back. I prefer the

---

[32] There are many successful actors who reportedly never went to drama school—the list includes Christian Bale, Jim Carrey, Russell Crowe, Tom Cruise, Johnny Depp, Cameron Diaz, Leonardo DiCaprio, Ben Kingsley, Heath Ledger, Jennifer Lawrence, Matthew McConaughey, Eddie Murphy, Joaquin Phoenix, Brad Pitt, Natalie Portman, Meg Ryan, and Charlize Theron (although this does not mean that they did not receive intensive and expensive acting coaching on set).

[33] The school has incredible alumni including Sir Laurence Olivier.

intimacy and honesty of the small screen. It is much easier to just … 'be'.

And so, because most people are exposed to the lives of other people through the news, films, and television, the power of acting ultimately depends on the authenticity of a performance and an audience's ability to accept a character—to again quote Bill Roache's definition of acting—'as true'. As an art, acting would be meaningless if not for the ability of an actor to engage an audience in this way. Indeed, there is something very powerful in seeing your story being told through a character whom you can relate to—and trust. (And as Bill says, "The Street" has always been rich in characters and this is as true today as it always was.') For this reason, generations of people all over the world have seen something of themselves and their lives in Ken Barlow and the residents of Coronation Street.

CHAPTER EIGHT

The Three Stages of Fame
'Time for Meditation and Contemplation'

Bill Roache is often described as one of 'Britain's most famous faces'. His popularity is even tracked four times a year by the social research organisation YouGov using nationally representative interviews. YouGov's interest raises two questions. The first is, what is fame? and the second, Why doesn't it mean very much to Bill?

Fame is the state of being known or talked about by many people, especially on account of some notable achievement. Celebrity is something different. Celebrity refers to someone who is celebrated because they are well-known, not necessarily on account of any achievement. In recent times, the ranks of the 'well-knowns' have dramatically expanded—but not for the better. Now the 'A-list' includes an eclectic pod of ne'er-do-wells, including the 'media personality', the 'influencer' and—at the bottom of the heap—the 'reality TV star', whose cynical creation was foreshadowed in a catalogue of Andy Warhol's work that mentioned, 'In the future everyone will be world-famous for 15 minutes,'[1] and more recently, in the movie *The Truman Show* (1998).[2]

The reality television format came to prominence in the early 2000s with the success of *Survivor, Idols,* and the *Big Brother* franchise, although *Candid Camera* (US) is considered the prototype.[3] However, the *Up* series (UK) is considered a better example of the more edifying possibilities for the genre.[4]

With few exceptions, the contemporary cult of celebrity has diluted the definition of authentic fame based on

---

[1] The expression was inspired by a quotation mis-attributed to Andy Warhol in a 1968 exhibition catalogue of his work at the Moderna Museet in Stockholm: 'In the future, everyone will be world-famous for 15 minutes.' The Museet Director was later quoted as saying, 'If he [Warhol] didn't say it, he could very well have said it. [So] Let's put it in.'

[2] *The Truman Show* broke new ground in film-making by exploring themes of existentialism, metaphilosophy, religion, simulated reality, and surveillance.

[3] The show aired in the US from 1948 until 2014. A UK version of the format aired from 1960 until 1976. It involved concealed cameras filming both celebrities and ordinary people being confronted with unusual situations, sometimes involving trick props. The joke was revealed by announcing the show's catchphrase, 'Smile, you're on *Candid Camera*.'

[4] The *Up* series is considered one of the best documentaries of all time. It follows the lives of 14 British children in England beginning in 1964, from the age of seven. The documentary has had nine episodes—one every seven years. The series was produced by Granada Television for ITV, except *42 Up* (1998), which was broadcast on BBC One.

achievement or merit. For example, both the eminent British naturalist Sir David Attenborough and the American Kim Kardashian are considered 'celebrities'— both are undeniably famous—however, one has made an incalculable contribution to the natural world and human society, the other, not so much. The writer Joseph Heller captured the absurdity of being famous for being famous in his acclaimed novel *Catch 22* as '… doing something of no benefit to anyone, more capably than anyone else'.

To compound this, the global media machine now cynically creates the human subjects as well as the topics of public conversation—conceivably brainstormed by privileged 'Gen X'ers' with man buns at round table editorial zooms. Many tabloid newspapers no longer even pretend to report the facts or reflect informed views but rather make it up and then set the terms of how the story will run based on 'the news cycle'—effectively advertising demand. This is another way of saying today's news is tomorrow's cod and chips wrapper, a lesson Bill Roache has learnt only too well.

Now, practically anyone can be a celebrity—and thus become famous—or infamous—because of it. And how do we know this? Facebook 'likes' and 'shares', 'trending tweets', 'hits' and 'unique web page views', have answered the question of whether fame can be objectively measured. (Before Facebook, an early unit of fame proposed by Erik Schulman in *The Annals of Improbable Research* (1999) was 'The Lewinsky', which has understandably been revised, as Ms Monica Lewinsky (Google her) is no longer so famous (or is that infamous)? But even this intriguing idea has darkened in the shade of fake news and Chinese 'click farms'.[5])

What attracts people to celebrity is a more difficult question to answer. One way to understand our relationship to public figures is what psychologists call projection. In part, this functions as a form of identification; we see in someone else those beliefs or ideas we would like to cultivate in ourselves and so we admire and over-empathise, and sometimes even 'worship' a celebrity because of it. (Note terms like 'American Idol' and 'Rock God' etc.) This, however, is not necessarily a bad thing.

For example, teenagers everywhere are inspired by the leadership of the teen Swedish climate activist Greta Thunberg. This is because her message gives them a sense of hope and purpose in a world that so often seems completely beyond their control. Stephen Hawking, the late renowned British theoretical physicist, was admired, not because people understood his contributions to physics but because his courageous struggle with motor neuron disease (amyotrophic lateral sclerosis) moved so many. Similarly, there were many gay people who felt validated and less isolated when Sir Elton John first spoke openly about his sexuality, and there are legions of Americans for whom the lyrics of Bruce Springsteen's songs resonate

---

[5] A click farm is a form of cyber fraud where sequenced mobile phones are programmed to electronically click on advertising links to boost their likes and shares.

with profound meaning, particularly the emotional and financial struggles associated with American working-class life.

So, given the potential impact of such identification, what does it *really* mean for Bill Roache to be authentically famous? Why is he admired? Certainly, he is best known for playing Ken Barlow in *Coronation Street* since 1960, but is there more to it than longevity in an acting role and the celebrity status of being 'a famous face?' (Or 'famous hair' as one journalist suggested—a trivial reference to Bill's full head of hair and a reflection of how shallow the media's take on celebrity has become).

Gerry O'Boyle, the—'well-known but not famous'—landlord of London's landmark jukebox joint, pub, and live music venue The Boogaloo, Highgate, offers a personal suggestion for another way of looking at Bill's fame.

As a young man, I sat with my Irish mother and we enjoyed the Coronation Street *storylines together—which often reflected some aspect of our own lives. And as an adult I am still following* Corrie—*and the one constant has been Bill Roache. I have a signed poster of Bill on the wall in the main bar. On my 50th birthday, Bill emailed me a lovely video. It went like this: 'Gerry, I want to wish you all the best for the first anniversary of your 49th birthday.' Very clever. And very kind. The measure of the man. We have never actually met in person but, as with many people in this country, Bill Roache has been in my life, and in my lounge room, for so long it feels like he is part of the family—and I suppose he is.*

Gerry O'Boyle's insight is mirrored by Bill's own perspective.

> Coronation Street *was conceived as social drama portraying the lives of ordinary people. It has never waved a flag, telling people what they should or shouldn't do, but many of its stories have reached out to people in need of support and I'm proud to have been a part of that. Over the years, we've had some fantastic storylines and that has helped raise awareness of important social issues too and, I hope, positively changed people's perceptions.*

It is important to recognise that Bill's perceptions have changed too because of his own experiences. Over more than six decades he has devised a guide to understanding how fame works—especially in his own life. He says, for him, there have been three stages.

The first is 'when fame is new and exciting, and the attention is enjoyed and appreciated'. Talking about the early days of *Coronation Street*, Bill says,

> *We were a television drama serial and highly respected. In less than a year we were top of the ratings. We were all instant stars with all that entailed.*

Fame and recognition came overnight. People like Tom Jones and the Beatles came to Granada to see us. Suddenly we were big stuff.

He further recounts the story of when he was invited to open a tearoom in the remote Orkney Islands as a favour to one of his army friends and the entire village turned out to see him. (And this was well before the invention of the World Wide Web [WWW] by British computer scientist Sir Tim Berners-Lee in 1989.)[6]

According to Bill, the villagers' curiosity and excitement is an example of the second stage of fame, 'When you are widely known, and you can never be "unknown" again and fame becomes claustrophobic, frightening and restrictive.'

The trouble is the media picked up on the Druidry and got pictures of me going around Stonehenge [in white robes] and that was it. 'He's a Druid.' This is the other side of fame—you can be subjected to intense media scrutiny at times … for this reason people tend to label you, and not always accurately, and I find labels are counterproductive—in fact harmful, because when people put you in a category, they restrict you and some will judge you or dislike you for it.

---

[6] Sir Timothy John Berners-Lee (born 8 June 1955) is an English computer scientist best known as the inventor of the World Wide Web. Berners-Lee devised an information management system in March 1989 and then implemented the first successful communication between a Hypertext Transfer Protocol HTTP client and server via the Internet in November of that same year.

The foil for Bill's second stage of fame is when people meet him in person. We had the good fortune of observing this dynamic at the launch of *The Pen y Gwryd Hotel: Tales from the Smoke Room*, where Bill was the special guest.[7] We watched as Bill put everyone in the room at ease with his charm and humility, and his obvious interest in listening to what others had to say. According to Bill, this is an example of the third stage of fame where, 'You simply learn to live with it.' As he says,

I am no better or no worse than anybody else just because I'm famous. I have a job that exposes me to the public and that's it. Fame doesn't mean a lot in terms of your state of being. If you take it too seriously and try to build on it too much in a way, it's dangerous. It is hard for people who get it for a short time and it's taken away from them before they can adjust to it; it is also hard if you get it too young. Fortunately, I have never been in a position of really letting it get to my head. Probably my background helped. The three years in repertory helped keep my feet on the ground. That was such a hard grind and I learned so much from my colleagues that there was no way I could get carried away with it. One of the advantages is the influence you can have. When Edwina died, we received a huge amount of support—letters from all over the country. Many were from people who

[7] Rob Goodfellow, Jonathan Copeland and Peter O'Neill, *The Pen y Gwryd Hotel: Tales from the Smoke Room*, Gomer, Llandysul Wales, 2016.

have suffered a similar loss and I felt I was able to share something with them.

Edwina was Bill and Sara Roache's second child. At the time, the comfort so many ordinary people experienced from such a well-known person openly sharing the tragic loss of an infant daughter was clearly appreciated. Later, Bill's interest in explaining his spiritual journey and speaking candidly about his personal philosophies likewise struck a chord with the public. This all seems very different to contemporary manifestations of fame that are clearly oriented towards image and money rather than kindness and community.

Bill's understanding of how to leverage his fame for the practical greater good was also characterised by his commitment to the Variety Club Golf society charity tournaments, and to his own golf classic, organised by Champions of Golf, which takes place at Nottingham's Rushcliffe Golf Club, which Bill started in 1991 to raise both awareness and funds for palliative care services.

Over the years, this has included East Cheshire Hospice in Macclesfield, Cheshire, Willow Wood Hospice in Ashton-under-Lyne, Lancashire, and Rainbows Hospice for Children and Young People in Loughborough, Leicestershire. As Nishil Saujani from Rainbows says,

In 1991, Bill became one of the first celebrities in the UK (and I suppose the world) to recognise that hospice care is a gift—a gift of a comfortable, dignified, and timely passing—a quiet revolution in our thinking about death and dying. And he has used his fame in the best possible way—to raise both awareness and funds. A wonderful legacy.

Bill has also been a strong supporter of the Seashell Trust, which supports children and young people with complex learning difficulties and special communication needs from across the UK (formerly the Royal School of the Deaf, Cheadle Hulme, Cheshire). As Dominic Tinner, relationship manager for Seashell commented,

I have fond memories of Bill and Sara visiting what was then called the Royal Schools for the Deaf, Manchester. They took a keen interest in our work with deaf young people with additional complex needs. It clearly left an impression on them as, when they were asked to appeal on ITV's All-Star Mr & Mrs, they chose to donate the proceeds to our charity.

In addition, Bill has raised funds for Brooke, an international charity that protects and improves the lives of working horses, donkeys and mules and gives people in the developing world a practical opportunity to work their way out of poverty.

*****

Bill Roache's fame now spans an incredible five generations. Dealing with being recognised wherever he goes is one thing, managing press attention is another. On the one hand, the media do not take kindly to celebrities who complain about celebrity—and benefit from it at the same time. (This is despite the general recognition of the destructive pressure of intense paparazzi scrutiny *à la* Princess Diana.) But denying the media access altogether can be fraught with its own considerable risks as Bill came to know better than anyone in Britain in the early 1990s with his libel case against *The Sun*.

Bill's lesson was, if you don't give an interview—and maintain some control over the questions being asked—a journalist is just as likely to make the entire thing up, which is effectively what happened. There is a saying in media management, 'The press can be like a pack of hungry wolves—if you don't give them something to eat, they may start looking at you as their next meal.' For some celebrity misfortunates, avoiding the media means never making direct eye contact in public or wearing a false beard, hat, and dark sunglasses, or employing strategies such as social isolation and even reclusiveness. And what is the point of that? In contrast, Bill seems to have found a happy medium, a third way, indeed a middle way, that others living in the 'the limelight' would do well to consider. As Bill says 'to live in the moment with the idea of love, always love' to keep him grounded.

These days, Bill lives on his own in Wilmslow, Cheshire, and is 'very happy with his own company', committed to playing the role of Ken Barlow until at least the age of 100. He enjoys frequent calls and visits from his children

Linus, James and Verity, and clearly benefits from the friendship of his manager John Hayes and the kindness of his confidants in Stride for Truth. Bill describes himself as 'completely fulfilled' and, further, that this is 'a wonderful position to be in'.

Since the relative peace of his two years as an Army Captain stationed in the Arabian desert, and then for most of his career in television, Bill Roache has yearned for time for 'meditation and contemplation' and for 'seeking the great truths that never change.' After a lifetime of professional acting, he has not only achieved merit-based recognition, but has also found quiet contentment beyond his fame as an individual. And, in these complicated, divisive, and troubled times, this is something to genuinely admire and aspire to.

CHAPTER NINE
Belief and Spirituality
Knowledge with a Capital 'K'

Throughout the second half of the 20th century, increased global travel and modern communications technology—from shortwave radio to the World Wide Web—has enabled us to learn about, and to experience first-hand, different cultures and their belief systems. For anyone seeking a fuller connection with this world (or the next for that matter), this has presented a rich smorgasbord of experiences, ideas, tastes, and textures. The world, it seemed, was waking up to itself. Why not refresh your thinking? Or broaden your lifestyle? Or even enhance your uniqueness as a human being? Or even explore the meaning of life?

The transition in British society from widespread formal religious affiliation to a much broader and richer spirituality is mirrored in the life of Bill

Roache.[1] His journey to overcome personal tragedy and discover the meaning of life reflects both change and continuity and reveals that post-Christian beliefs, in a historically Christian society, can be both complex and intriguing. It also reinforces the idea that something can be real for one person, like belief, but cannot be empirically measured by another.[2]

For over 35 years, the UK's leading independent (not for profit) social research agency—the National Centre for Social Research (NatCen)—has conducted an annual survey that includes questions about religion and belief. NatCen's data on religious affiliation from their annual British Social Attitudes Survey reveals enormous intergenerational changes in British society.[3] According to NatCen, the proportion of 'non-believers' has increased gradually but progressively since the survey began in 1983. For example, the proportion of people in Britain who describe themselves as having 'no religion' is now at its highest level ever. In fact, more than half of the British people surveyed currently describe themselves in this way.

---

[1] The Church of England effectively came into existence in 1534 because Henry Vlll decided to break away from the dominant religious institution. Why? Because the Catholic Pope would not permit him to divorce his wife so that he could marry another woman.

[2] Rob Goodfellow, Dawn O'Neil and Peter Smith, *Saving Face, Losing Face, In Your Face: A Journey into the Western Heart, Mind and Soul*, Butterworth Heinemann, Oxford, 1999.

[3] Curtice, J., Clery, E., Perry, J., Phillips M. and Rahim, N. (eds.) (2019), *British Social Attitudes: The 36th Report, London: The National Centre for Social Research*. bsa.natcen.ac.uk/latest-report/british-social-attitudes-36/religion.aspx

This decline appears most dramatically in respect of the Church of England, with only 15% of Britons now considering themselves to be Anglican—half the number who claimed this affiliation at the turn of the millennium. Interestingly, over the last 30 years, the proportion of people describing themselves as Roman Catholic has remained relatively stable—at around one in ten—with a mere 6% of people across the UK belonging to non-Christian religions—such as Islam, Hinduism, Sikhism, Judaism and Buddhism—in that order.

However, there is also good evidence that, despite the falling popularity of formal or organised religion, most people in the UK still believe in a higher power, as Bill Roache does. Complementing NatCen's report, a study commissioned by the Christian think tank Theos, and undertaken by the London-based ComRes's Faith Research Centre, recorded that 77% of the British people believe that there are things, 'that cannot be explained by reason or science'. This included 8% of respondents who said they, or someone they knew, had experienced a miracle. Likewise, from an early age, Bill demonstrated a sense of purpose that could not be explained by reason alone. As a boy growing up in Ilkeston, this feeling was so strong that he resolved to become a missionary doctor in China. As he says,

A sense of destiny, a vocation, or a mission … call it what you will. I knew I would recognise my purpose in life when I saw it and devote myself wholeheartedly to its fulfilment.

To say that Bill hailed from a non-conformist religious background is an understatement. A better description would be eccentric, even eclectic. He was brought up on stories about his grandfather Dr William Hugh Roache who, according to him, had a reputation for an 'open-minded approach to all things hidden and mysterious'—including hypnotism, alternative medicine (homeopathy), spiritualism and theosophy.[4]

Dr William Hugh Roache also had an interest in the teachings of Rudolf Steiner,[5] an Austrian philosopher, social reformer, architect, economist and esotericist. In 1934, this led him and Edith Lewis (the daughter of the Meridian Hosiery Factory proprietor J.B. Lewis)[6] to establish a Steiner School in the grounds of the Roache family home. Called Michael House, the school was charged with teaching an alternative system of holistic education that aimed to develop, 'the head, hand and heart'. According to Bill,

Rudolf Steiner schools work towards developing harmonised individuals, with music and art regarded as of equal value to academic facts.

---

[4] Theosophy is derived from the Greek words theos (God) and sophia (or divine wisdom). It is the idea that knowledge of the supernatural can be achieved through direct experience, intuition, or revelation. The Theosophical Society was founded in the US in 1875 by Helena Blavatsky but formed factions with the most widespread international group now headquartered in India.

[5] In the 1920s, Steiner invented the concept of biodynamic farming to counter the rise of synthetic fertilisers.

[6] nottshistory.org.uk/books/nottsillus1898/textiles11.htm

The two-and-a-half years that Bill was at Michael House were the happiest of all his school days. Steiner (also called Waldorf) education had laid an unconventional lifelong foundation in ways of thinking and interpreting the world—including what he refers to as 'an implicit spiritual ethos'.

And as Bill has further said,

> *What we learnt more than anything else was to care for other people and take responsibility for our own actions. Strangely, discipline was not needed, as it seemed almost out of place to misbehave. There was a feeling of harmony that no one wanted to disrupt, and there was kindness and patience from the teachers which dissolved all aggression. It was a memorable and colourful experience that no doubt helped to nurture the seeds that would later flower into spiritual awareness.*

Detractors of the Steiner curriculum argue that this ethos—called anthroposophy (or 'special educational insights into childhood development') is underpinned by concealed forms of mysticism characterised by a belief in *karma*. This is where both current and past individual actions—both good and bad—influence the nature and quality of reincarnations. On the other hand, adherents of anthroposophy maintain that their philosophy offers children a balanced 'mind, body, soul and spirit pathway of understanding' incorporating the existence of an objective and comprehensible spiritual world. Notwithstanding arguments for or against Steiner education, these 'truths' would later feature prominently in Bill's life.

By the age of seven, and the first year of boarding school, the die had been cast for the young Bill Roache—echoing the Jesuit maxim 'Give me a child until he is seven and I will give you the man,' which itself is based on the much earlier quote by Aristotle 'Give me a child until he is seven and I will show you the man.' (The former was an ideology—the latter an observation.) This ingrained spirituality was complicated by a near paralysing fear of death and an equally pervasive preoccupation with eternity. As Bill says,

> *Death seemed so final, so awful. Being a somewhat shy, introverted boy, I couldn't express this terror, and it stayed with me as I matured into adolescence.*

> *I went from awe, to fear, to absolute panic when I thought about this—infinity—and it reached a stage where I couldn't look up at the sky. The stars were too meaningful, too frightening.*

> *It was the fear of death that drove me to search beyond the normal channels for the truth about life and death and it was the fear of infinity that showed me there was more to life than could be understood by our finite minds.*

> *My fear of death and infinity caused me to seek truth and understanding. For this reason, I am eternally grateful to them.*

Not surprisingly, as a sensitive young man in his final year at Rydal School (just before National Service), his favourite subjects were not the prerequisites to study medicine, as his father and grandfather had, but rather English, history and scripture—which, in his own words 'seemed to better qualify me to be a vicar rather than a doctor'. However, the answers to his many questions about the existence of a God, who would 'allow wars, disease, poverty, torture, and loneliness', were brushed aside by the school's chaplain—with evasive platitudes such as 'God works in mysterious ways' and, 'It's best to rely on belief and faith.' For Bill, this was countered by one question: 'what is the purpose of it all?'

Significantly, Bill's Steiner foundations were to later lead him to reject the chaplain's advice and instead look for what he calls 'knowledge with a capital K'—knowledge of a universal truth, a plan, and a purpose to life. This included an introduction to a medium at a spiritualist meeting in his early 20s (although he comments that his motivation at the time was more attuned to an interest in a living girl than communication with the dead).

The next chapter in Bill's spiritual journey was written on the Pirate Coast of the Arabian Peninsula during his time in the British Army. For nearly two years, Bill was in command of a contingent of Bedouin troops—warriors drawn from the seven sheikhdoms of the Persian Gulf. His mission was to play a role in keeping the peace in what was broadly called the 'Al Buraimi Oasis Dispute'—a long-running regional feud between nomadic tribes—

where, according to Bill, 'One wrong move and we had an international incident on our hands.' After promotion to the rank of Captain, his commanding officer briefed him on his desert mission accordingly.

The squadron is made up of 140 Arabs, none of whom speak any English. You have a week to know the language. By the way, the previous commander was shot by his own men. Any questions?

Captain Roache's management of a delicate military standoff at the Oasis was to earn his squadron a letter of congratulations from then Prime Minister, Anthony Eden.[7]

Stationed in a remote outpost called Mirfa in the *Rub' al Khali*—or 'Empty Quarter' of the Arabian Desert—(the largest sand desert in the world), the posting was, as Bill says, 'a near Biblical existence' as well as an opportunity for long periods of 'untutored meditation'. In his autobiographies, he describes the calming effect of the vast wilderness and how cool and peaceful it was in the evenings. For Bill, the nights were especially suitable for contemplation on the direction life was taking him, and how he felt about God and religion. One can imagine the not-so-distant echoes of another British

---

[7] In the British Army a squadron was historically a company-sized military formation. The term is still used to refer to modern cavalry units but can also be used as a designation for other arms and services. All squadron commanders must be the rank of Captain or above.

Officer, Thomas Edward (T.E.) Lawrence, CB, DSO (1888–1935)—'Lawrence of Arabia'—and the mystical influence that the desert clearly had on both men.

Those who went into the desert long enough to forget its open spaces and its emptiness were inevitably thrust upon God as the only refuge and rhythm of being.

T.E. Lawrence, *Seven Pillars of Wisdom.*

As with Michael House in Albion (as the island of Britain was once called), the Arabian desert also left its mark on Bill.[8] Evidence of this is that during his early *Coronation Street* days, he had a reputation for exploring the supernatural, from 'table-rapping' (communicating with the dead akin to the use of a Ouija board during a séance), clairvoyance (predicting future events), astrology and even Druidry. According to him,

Looking for the truth sounds simple, but how many people can rid themselves of bias, prejudice, opinions, belief, faith—all the trappings picked up as we go through life—and assess them objectively? Studying with the Druids was only one step on the path of my quest for greater knowledge. How many people can strip themselves clean and approach new ideas with a fresh look?

---

[8] *Alba* in Scottish Gaelic, *Albain* (genitive *Alban*) in Irish, *Nalbin* in Manx and *Alban* in Welsh and Cornish.

It is at this point in the story where Bill's post-Christian Aquarian beliefs become especially interesting—and even more complex than they may appear—even to him. Indeed, throughout his books you can find references to what the American blogger Aaron Loy calls, 'the undomesticated Sermon on the Mount'—or the unvarnished teachings of Jesus.[9] For example, in *Ken and Me,* Bill quotes what he himself refers to as an 'ancient adage'—namely, 'Ask and it will be given you. Seek, and you will find. Knock, and the door will be opened for you' (Matthew 7:7).[10] Bill also talks about his personal spiritual journey as a quest for 'The Holy Grail', about his life in the acting profession as 'a mission', and about his belief in 'creation'.

> *Maybe we were just a chemical accident, as the atheists believe—animals who have reached a certain level of intellectual capacity through the trial and error of evolution. I couldn't really accept that. It makes everything seem so pointless and futile. You only have to look at the complexity of a flower, or the birth of a baby … to see there is definitely a plan and a purpose.*

---

[9] The 'Age of Aquarius' is represented by the water bearer, the mystical healer who bestows life. Aquarius is regarded by astrologists as the most humanitarian of the astrological signs. The idea of an Age of Aquarius entered popular culture in the 1960s and 1970s with the New Age/hippy movement and was popularised by the 1967 musical *Hair,* with its opening song 'Aquarius'.

[10] The Sermon on the Mount is set out in the Christian Bible in chapters five to seven of the Gospel of Matthew. The traditional setting for what is the longest teaching in the Christian Bible is the Mount of Beatitudes, a hill on the Korazim Plateau in northern Israel.

The conclusion—Bill has seemingly escaped 'goldfish bowl religion' or the restraints imposed by powerful institutions, unchallenged traditions, and self-serving vested interests. This shows throughout his writings— from the questions he asks in *Ken and Me* (1993) to his dedicated search for truth in *Soul on the Street* (2007) and *50 Years on the Street: My Life with Ken Barlow* (2010) and on to his maturing personal spirituality in his bestselling book, *Life and Soul: How to Live a Long and Healthy Life* (2018). For Bill,

> *Our chattering minds and turbulent emotions must be bypassed to see reality for what it is.*

At one point in the early 1970s, Bill briefly referred to his affiliation with the Church of England but, at that time, he was clearly in the process of evaluating his position as, according to data from NatCen's survey, have many other British people.

> *The established church has become lost in sectarian and theological argument and is no longer spiritually based ... the message of Christ was simple: love and forgiveness.*

For many years, Bill studied under a spiritual guide—the homeopathist and former Chief Druid of The Ancient Order of Druids[11] (1964–1976) Dr Thomas Lackenby

---

[11] The Ancient Order of Druids has counted as members important public figures such as Sir Winston Churchill, the slavery abolitionist Sir Charles James Fox and the novelist William Makepeace Thackery.

Maughan.[12] Maughan borrowed from a wide swathe of ideas including Buddhism and Hinduism, but was also interested in anthroposophy, spiritualism, and theosophy. However, meditation, philanthropy and brotherly love were considered his main areas of interest. As Bill said of his spiritual mentor,

> *He explained that the whole point of being here was to develop spiritually and then be of service to others. Basically, that was it. It was wonderfully simple.*

And in respect of the practice of meditation that Maughan taught,

> *Meditation is essential to spiritual development. It can also help with all other aspects of life too. At the lowest level it can reduce stress, anxiety, tension, and worry. At the highest level it enables you to tune in to your soul. The main purpose of meditation is to quieten the mental, emotional, and physical aspects of oneself, thus allowing a greater contact with the higher, or spiritual, self.*

---

[12] Maughan was a colourful character who, in describing himself, once said, 'La human being is a loosely connected bunch of ill-assorted attributes.' Various sources place him as a Royal Navy veteran of the First World War, who then fought against fascism in the Spanish Civil War and served in Naval Intelligence in the Second World War. In the 1950s, he travelled extensively in the Himalayas and assisted the Dalai Lama in evacuating monks from Tibet to India following the Chinese invasion in March 1959.

Overall, Bill's experiences correspond to what the religious writer Brandon Vogt refers to as the 'lapsed Catholic experience', namely 'spiritual but not religious', or to those who reject doctrine and dogma, or formal religion, but still believe in a higher power and still pray—and, as is the case with Bill Roache, and many of his generation, who continue to refer to the Bible as a way of understanding themselves and explaining the world. For example, he says,

When Jesus was tempted in the wilderness the devil told him he could have all the material things he wanted. He had that choice and overcame it. We all have that choice too.

Today Bill makes it clear that he has made such a choice and has, 'no connection with any church'. What he does have, however, is a strong connection with the idea of 'God, peace and love for all'—which is exemplified in the acceptance, kindness and support he has received from members of the Manchester-based 'Circle of Love' now known as 'Stride for Truth'.

Founded by Ann Rogers, a retired nurse, Stride for Truth is a modest support group that claims to encompass all faiths, religions, and nationalities, and is characterised by friendly open discussions about meditation and spirituality. Ann simply calls it 'a team of people'. The group's stated beliefs are simple: 'pure love conquers all' (as is their mission) and 'working with God for love and peace—treating others with acceptance—the way you yourself would like to be treated.' Again, there are echoes of the teachings of Jesus here,

> *A new commandment I give unto you, that ye love one another; as I have loved you, that ye also love one another.*

> *By this shall all men know that ye are my disciples, if ye have love one to another.*

John 13:34–35 King James Version (KJV).

And directly quoting the Jewish scriptures, or *Tanakh* (Leviticus 19:18) Jesus reminds the gathered multitude of The Golden Rule,

> *And as ye that men should do to you, do ye also to them likewise.*

(Luke 6:31) (KJV).

These ideas are, however, by no means exclusively Christian, or Jewish for that matter; rather similar precepts can be found, according to the American Egyptologist John Albert Wilson, as far back as the Late Period (c.664–323 BCE) in a papyrus i.e, 'That which you hate to be done to you, do not do to another', as well as in subtle variations across all the world's great religious traditions, faiths, and beliefs. In fact, The Golden Rule is now regarded as a 'global ethic' or what many, including Bill call, 'a universal truth'—one based on the human qualities of compassion, empathy, forgiveness, kindness, love, respect and understanding.[13]

Frequent references to the Bible are not surprising for someone of Bill's generation—regardless of his direct criticisms of the established Church and despite his New Age beliefs. Like most of the Traditionalist generation, Bill was brought up on Sunday school, given formal secondary school religious instruction, and memorised the Apostles' Creed, (which affirms belief in God the Father, Jesus Christ His Son, and the Holy Spirit), the Lord's Prayer and The Golden Rule—all of which continue to inform his world view, consciously or subconsciously, as they may also do for many who claimed 'no religion' in the NatCen survey. The teachings of Jesus clearly remain one of Bill's moral compass coordinates—including notions of what is good and bad, what is right and wrong, and what is fitting.

An example of this is that his life does not mirror that of many other celebrities—including contemporary actors, athletes, pop stars and reality television personalities, who appear to be incapable of curbing their self-seeking excesses. Indeed, celebrity extravagance is frequently exploited for blatant publicity, and to deflect personal

---

[13] In 1993, the *Declaration Toward a Global Ethic* from the Parliament of the World's Religions proclaimed The Golden Rule as a common principle of 143 major world faiths, including the Baha'i Faith, Brahmanism, Brahma Kumaris, Buddhism, Christianity, Hinduism, Interfaith, Islam, Jainism, Judaism, Native American, Neo-Paganism, Sikhism, Taoism, Theosophy, Unitarian Universalism and Zoroastrianism.

accountability—something that Bill Roache could never be accused of. The tragedies in Bill's life—such as the death of his infant daughter Edwina in 1984 aged 18 months (from acute bronchial pneumonia), the death of his wife Sara on 7 February 2009 age 58 (from cardiac arrest), and the passing of his eldest daughter Vanya on 2 March 2018 age 50 (from liver failure)—have firmly grounded him, like most so-called 'ordinary' human beings, in the gritty reality of everyday life. (Bill says he is still grieving for his *Coronation Street* co-star Anne Kirkbride, who played Deirdre Barlow for 42 years, and who died on 19 January 2015—aged 60 from breast cancer.)

Particularly poignant are the circumstances surrounding Sara Roache's death, which was unusually tragic and traumatic—her heart suddenly stopped as she was lying next to her husband chatting. The corollary? Given the grief Bill has endured, his beliefs are not as unusual as they could otherwise seem.

To illustrate this, a context for Bill's personal spirituality can be found in the story of Jonny Kennedy (1966–2003)—the subject of the Emmy award-winning Channel 4 documentary, *The Boy Whose Skin Fell Off* (and a book of the same name by Roger Stutter). Both record the final months of Kennedy's life and his subsequent death from medical complications of the dreadful inherited condition recessive dystrophic epidermolysis bullosa.

In the film, Kennedy, who had a very personal and individual view on faith and religion, ('a bit of a pick and mix' as he says in the film), talks about his impending death as, 'a freedom … a lesson … and an escape'.

Just before he died at the age of 36, Kennedy explained it in this way,

I know inside that there is more to life than this mortal coil. It's a very shallow-minded person who thinks that someone is born and dies and that's it. I haven't gone through 30-odd years of suffering, and doing what I do, and looking at other people who are born and die with cancer, with AIDS, with whatever, and think, 'Well, what was the point of that?' There is a point to everything, and we're here to learn, and it's just a learning curve and we'll move on, and this is just a shell. It's just I've got a dodgy shell.

Bill says something very similar. 'You are in the world but not of it. The body is the temple of the spirit.' Such beliefs were clearly real to Jonny Kennedy as well. Likewise, the trusted friendships cultivated in Stride for Truth have given Bill the strength to bear his own loss and grief and, as such, his beliefs—and those of Jonny Kennedy for that matter—are at least worthy of respect, if not serious investigation. And given the influences on Bill's formative years—from Michael House to the Arabian Desert—his commitment to the Manchester-based group would seem to be an understandable progression in his lifelong quest for truth or as Bill prefers to say, knowledge with a capital 'K'—'working with God to bring freedom, free will, love, peace, and truth to this troubled world'.

CHAPTER TEN
Life and Longevity
Flourishing in the Third Age

On 25 April 2032, Bill Roache will be officially 100 years old, although, until the age of 18, he celebrated his birthday on 23 April, the result of misplaced birth records in a long-demolished maternity hospital in Basford, Nottingham.[1] And so, he has the distinction of having both a real birth date—the 23rd—and an official birthday—the 25th.

Bill's family birthday tradition is for the 'birthday boy' or 'girl' to be greeted in the morning by a display of balloons, happy birthday banners, best wishes cards and presents. Later, the Roache family goes out to dinner where there is

---

[1] Fatefully for Bill Roache's future career on *Coronation Street*, for many years, the largest industry in Basford was soap manufacturing. In 2005, in a sign of the times, the Cussons Sons & Co soap factory was closed and production moved to Thailand.

always a specially designed cake served at the end of the meal. This is followed by a family walk and a 'Face Time' with Linus Roache in New York.

According to the UK Office for National Statistics, on that day in 2032, Bill will share the distinction of living for 100 years with nearly 90,000 other inhabitants of the British Isles. Some demographers have even suggested that, by mid-century, there will be three centenarians for every newborn. This trend is mirrored in other places where *Coronation Street* and the character of Ken Barlow remain immensely popular—such as Australia, Canada, South Africa, and Aotearoa New Zealand. For example, between the years 2000 and 2020, the number of Australians aged 85 and over grew by 110% compared with national population growth of 35%. This means that a baby girl (or is that a 'sheila'?) born today has a 40% greater chance of reaching the age of 100—with Aussie men not far behind.

In the UK and elsewhere, this change has put enormous pressure on everything from state pension budgets to the provision of nursing home services, not to mention competition for assisted care and walking frame-friendly berths on international touring cruise ships. Although, as the American baseball player, Yogi Berra, once famously advised, 'It's tough to make predictions, especially about the future.' And this is particularly true of the Covid-19 pandemic which has so dramatically changed our world.

To put this demographic tsunami into perspective, when Queen Elizabeth II ascended the throne in 1952 (with the Coronation on 2 June 1953 at Westminster Abbey), Her Majesty continued the tradition established by her grandfather King George V of sending congratulatory messages to UK centenarians with only hand-delivered telegrams dispatched—not letters as it is today—and certainly not emails, texts, or tweets. King George V also sent out letters of congratulations to British couples celebrating their 60th wedding anniversary, a tradition his direct heir, King Edward VIII, and his American wife, Wallis Simpson of Baltimore, for some reason, chose not to continue.

These days, a dedicated centenarian team in Whitehall's Department for Work and Pensions (the UK's largest public service department) is responsible for managing the Monarch's recognition of her most venerable subjects who, to use a cricketing term, have reached '100 not out'. The process is: Buckingham Palace sends a card on behalf of Her Majesty and then the centenarian team (unless otherwise requested by the celebrant) sends another on behalf of the Secretary of State for Work and Pensions. In recent years, for example, according to records, Her Majesty sent over 6,000 cards annually in recognition of individual 100th birthdays.

The projection of 90,000 British centenarians by 2032 represents a staggering 355-fold increase in just three generations. Her Majesty will herself be 100 years old on 21 April 2026—which is her real birthday, as opposed to a plethora of official regal birthdays celebrated across the Commonwealth.[2] (And it was a milestone Her Majesty's own mother, the late Queen Elizabeth, The Queen Mother, reached on 4 August 2000.)

As for Bill Roache, he is on the public record as confirming his intention to continue working as an actor until 'the age of 120—if possible', making him a 'supercentenarian', i.e. those aged 110 and over—although, as always, Ken Barlow's fate remains in the hands of the ITV scriptwriters who from time to time have threatened to 'kill him off'. Examples are when he suffered and then recovered from a stroke (October 2016); or when he was pushed down the stairs of his home at 1 Coronation Street by a mystery assailant as part of a marathon whodunnit plot (March 2017 extending to May 2017). The culprit was revealed to be Ken's own grandson Daniel—with the storyline concluding in June 2017 after an incredible 53 episodes.

These storylines make the fictional Ken Barlow a survivor of the unhappy trio of a cerebrovascular accident (or stroke), elder abuse and a fall and also being both a

---

[2] Queen Elizabeth's official birthday is primarily celebrated with Trooping the Colour—over 1,400 parading soldiers, 200 horses and 400 musicians coming together in a display of military precision, horsemanship, and fanfare to mark the occasion. Royal Salutes are also fired from various locations across the UK. In London, salutes are fired both from the Tower of London and either Hyde Park or Green Park. The basic salute is 21 rounds, fired at 10 second intervals, but in Hyde Park an extra 20 shots are fired because it is a Royal Park. The Queen's private birthday is often spent with family and friends behind closed doors at one of the royal residences.

'delayer' and 'escaper', to use the professional jargon, of conditions like cancer, dementia, diabetes, heart disease, high blood pressure, kidney disease, and osteoporosis (though not Covid-19 which Bill Roache contracted in real life and made a complete recovery from in 2021). All are typical conditions experienced by many who live to very old age. As Caroline Abrahams, Charity Director at Age UK, has said,

> *The growing number of older people in the UK is a cause for real celebration. However, increased lifespan alone is not a measure of progress. People in later life don't simply want to live longer, they also want to live better. For this to happen, we all need to help break down ageist barriers that turn older people into second-class citizens and instead build a world where they can be prioritised and flourish.*

With so many dedicating themselves to empowering older people to maintain active and meaningful lives, the issues to consider are: with a quarter of the children born in Britain today expected to reach 100 years of age, what can we learn from Bill's rich life and great longevity? How do the twilight years of this famous man reflect changes in British society? In what way has Bill himself challenged the currently accepted three stages of life—namely, 'education' (between the ages of five and 21), 'work' (between 22 and 65) and 'retirement'—or the Third Age (from the age of 65 onwards). And finally, what do Bill's experiences tell us about growing old and keeping well—or 'flourishing?'

Many of the answers to these questions can be found in Bill's book *Life and Soul* in which his 'thoughts and actions' on these subjects feature prominently. As he says,

> *My aim was to share some of the truths and practices for physical and spiritual well-being I have learned along the way.*

*****

David Sinclair, Director of the International Longevity Centre UK, significantly reminds us that, 'Today's young are tomorrow's older people.' Casting back to 1960, the fictional Ken Barlow was youth personified—eager, hopeful, and idealistic. Typical of his generation, the young Barlow pushed the boundaries of almost everything and his conservative-minded fictional *Coronation Street* father pushed right back, as did the entire establishment—working-class, middle-class, and elite alike. Nowhere is this narrative friction better illustrated than in an episode of *Coronation Street* that aired on 12 February 1962.

As foreshowed in our introduction, the scene is set in the cavern-like original Rovers Return Inn. What begins as a public contest of different world views ends in a very physical confrontation between the newly graduated high school teacher—Ken Barlow, and the older Second World War veteran Len Fairclough (Peter Adamson), a metaphor for the turbulent and combative 1960s.

After aggressively 'shirt fronting' Barlow (an antipodean term popularised by former Australian Prime Minister and one-time boxer Tony Abbott), a seriously annoyed Fairclough begins his diatribe in his typically thick, idiom-rich, working-class Lancashire accent.

> *He [Barlow] might be a walkin', flamin' dictionary, but 'e 'asn't the guts of a louse.*

Fairclough continues, seemingly addressing his tirade to Barlow, while really appealing to his constituency of like-minded drinkers and, of course, tens of millions of older, sympathetic British viewers.

> *Look, if there's one thing wrong with Coronation Street it's because it sometimes throws up nasty, clever dicks like you. So, belt off home and get your daddy to change your nappy before you get hurt!*

Then it gets (more) personal—quickly, regrettably as things do today in the Facebook-enabled 'age of rage'—as Fairclough creates an even sharper distinction between the generations.

> *There is one little thing you don't seem to understand Kenneth Barlow and that's the fact that Harry and me were scrapping for you during the war … you know … with rifles and bayonets and that kind'a stuff. But you wouldn't understand that, would you? We hadn't time to write articles—did we Harry? I suppose you'd just stand there and let 'em all come.*

The popular public house landlord, Jack Walker (Arthur Leslie) steps in as the lonely voice of reason.

Ay, ay, ay! That's enough lad!

But it's too late—youth and new thinking are on a collision course with age and reaction as Ken Barlow replies directly and fearlessly to the indignant, heavy-set house builder.

That's just the kind of intelligent reaction I'd expect from a loud-mouthed, beer-swilling, moron like you!

Clearly Ken Barlow is speaking to a different community of *Coronation Street* viewers from those following Len Fairclough's wordy indignation. There is now no room for compromise and the scene ends in the much-celebrated fist fight, with the two men crashing through a broken door and lurching back again into the public bar, with Len Fairclough storming out with a muttering scrum of his like-minded drinking mates while the seemingly unconscious Ken Barlow—who is not faring too badly under the circumstances—is smothered by three comforting, concerned and consoling, attractive young women.

Over half a century later, it is the baby boomers and those on the generational cusp—or the traditionalists (anyone born before the end of the Second World War)—who are again taking control of an agenda for change. And, as in 1960, Bill Roache and his alter ego Ken Barlow remain typical of the aspirations of their age; but this time they both represent an ascendant older generation who are pushing the boundaries of everything from work-life balance to sexuality—and significantly controlling not only the financial means to shape their respective futures but also the circumstances of their retirement.

A wonderful example of the latter can be seen in the landmark 10,000th episode of *Coronation Street* broadcast in February 2020. This ended in the shock revelation that Ken Barlow was voluntarily leaving 'The Street' to move into a plush retirement home with his girlfriend Claudia Colby (Rula Lenska). In typically dramatic fashion, as Ken Barlow walks his dog Eccles at the end of the episode, he speaks directly to the rain-moistened, dimly lit cobblestone street that has become so much a part of British popular culture: '80 years too late, but finally it's time to go. Goodbye old friend.'

The following episode sees Ken Barlow break the news to his family, with his children Peter and Tracy immediately squabbling over who will get his house—reflecting the tensions so often associated with the intergenerational division of assets. Not surprisingly, fans could not imagine 'The Street' without him and on 22 April 2020, the scriptwriters obliged and Ken Barlow 'dropped a bombshell' (as the tabloids described it) on Claudia and not only declared that he was leaving the five-star Stillwaters retirement complex—and moving back to 'the cobbles'—but leaving her as well. Gulp!

In 2020, and at the age of 80, the fictional Ken Barlow was clearly making his own decisions. And in 2022, at the real age of 90, Bill Roache himself exudes this same sense of direction, purpose and vitality as he challenges the entrenched idea that age automatically means physical and intellectual decline. The British tabloid press refer to Bill as 'remarkable' and 'well preserved'. They even use that old cliché—'good for his age.' However, in his mind, this accolade extends well beyond mere physical appearance as he clearly embraces a much more meaningful journey of personal and spiritual growth. He describes this as being,

Forward looking and being optimistic, often working towards goals and being part of something greater than yourself.

Bill is, in fact, an exemplar of generational group thinking (as he was as a young actor in the early 1960s). Truly, there is no one quite like him. He was and remains a dominating individual who characterises the age more than any other actor in the UK today. And, although his cohort of fellow travellers are clearly no longer the younger generation, they still have a strong sense of themselves and of their potential. As Bill says,

When enough of us know how to truly live, we too will reach a tipping point—we'll create a shift in consciousness that will create happier, healthier, and longer lives.

For the children and grandchildren of Bill's generation, this advice comes with a sobering qualification. While the immediate post-Second World War generation may be the wealthiest in history (estimated to be worth £25 trillion globally), their eager and excitable heirs should not count on getting their hands on the *moola*—because living a long, healthy, and happy life can come with a hefty price tag. Rather, the very best that Generation X (born between 1965 and 1976), the on-the-cusp Xennials, those with an analogue childhood and a digital adulthood (born 1977–1983), the Millennials (born 1983–1995), the Centennials (born after 1996), and now Generation Z, or the cohort succeeding the Millennials, can expect, when the smoke and debris of the grow old disgracefully revolution (think Eddy and Patsy from *Absolutely Fabulous*) finally clears in a maelstrom of empty Stolichnaya bottles, are small, fragmented and wait for it … drained inheritances. (Actually, even this prediction may prove to be overly optimistic.)

Bill Roache's sensible advice to those who are either enjoying their wealth or alternately, impatiently waiting for a juicy inheritance is,

> *Not to feel stressed about future outcomes and instead just focus on what you are doing right now.*

In his book *Life and Soul: How to Live a Long and Healthy Life*, Bill talks about an approach that typifies his attitude to work. He explains that when he prepares for a scene on *Coronation Street*, instead of looking at the script and thinking, 'I'll never learn all of this,' he takes the first page and tackles the first few words. And that—according to him—is 'all it takes to get myself going'. This very practical expression of mindfulness ensures that he is productive— despite the digital 'age of distraction'. There is a name for this—the 'leading edge'. The analogy is a table that is too heavy to lift; what you can do is be mindful enough to at least take hold of the leading edge. The idea is that the hardest part is just starting (and then someone might see you struggling and even offer to help).

Psychologists say that what Bill is doing represents a healthy approach to ageing because mindfulness can break the cycle of overthinking—or as some people say 'stewing' over things that are beyond our control such as growing old or being overwhelmed with memorising new scripts for that matter. As Bill says,

In learning script lines, as in life, focusing on what you are doing is far more important than worrying about the future.

In what could easily become an anthem for the older generation, Bill's personal leitmotif for well-being is, 'moderation, commonsense and enjoyment'. This sounds simple enough when, in fact, the idea of well-being is a complex interplay of genetic (biological), psychological, socio-economic, and cultural factors. And it has a long history. The first major statement on the importance of well-being can be found in the preamble to the constitution of the World Health Organisation (1948).

Health is a state of complete physical, mental, and social well-being and not merely the absence of disease or infirmity.

Since 1948, there have been some serious scientific efforts as well as waves of popular ideas about what it means to live well. In contrast, an entire global industry has been built around the concept of wellness, with commercial interests peddling everything from miracle balms to magnetised mattresses. Significantly, wellness does not have a definition that everyone can agree on. It is like the difference between 'counsellor' and 'psychologist'.

A psychologist is a trained and certified professional. In contrast, there is no restriction on the title counsellor, which can be used by anybody—and often is. Well-being then is an established area of research in psychology, whereas some critics suggest that wellness is little more than a marketing strategy. The problem is that academics have struggled to capture what well-being means as well. For example, the distinguished psychologist Martin Seligman, who founded the positive psychology movement, developed a model of well-being based on the concept of 'flourishing'—from the Greek word *eudaimonia*, which broadly translates to 'living the good life'.

Seligman said that there are five elements necessary for well-being, namely positive emotions, engagement, relationships, meaning, purpose, and accomplishment. And it is at this point that the readers of *Life and Soul* begin to get the idea that Bill Roache, while by no means a trained psychologist, is pretty much on the money as far as flourishing is concerned.

Another view of well-being was proposed by psychologist Edward F. Diener. 'Diener's tripartite model of subjective well-being'—a frightening set of words, but a simple enough concept—looks at a balance of positive experiences, negative experiences, and life evaluation. Again, we see this in Bill's reflection on both personal growth and professional success.

We likewise see in his life a third idea called 'Ryff's multi-dimensional model of well-being'. Again, a mouthful but important to understanding where Bill is coming from. This identifies self-acceptance, personal growth, purpose in life, environmental mastery (or, in other words, coping with things), autonomy (or just being independent) and good relations with others as the keys to well-being. (Psychologists love to use overly complex language as a way of making their ideas seem original.)

Clearly, trying to distil well-being into a set of concrete concepts is almost impossible without losing much of the complexity and nuance of life. However, it is conceivable to discern a core set of basic principles from the life of Bill Roache that broadly cover both well-being and successful ageing, namely,

Keep your body and mind active, be helpful to others, and have a purpose bigger than yourself that gives your life meaning. That's it!

Interestingly, like well-being, there is no universal definition for what has been coined 'successful ageing'. However, as far back as 1987, two researchers, John Rowe and Robert Khan, proposed that successful ageing involved, 'engagement with life'—or social contact and participation in productive activities such as paid (or for that matter volunteer) work. More recently, others such as Martha Crowther, have included 'positive spirituality' as part of an enhanced model for successful ageing and it is this that Bill, together with some commonsense approaches to good physical health, most identifies as responsible for his general flourishing.

*****

As Bill says, full time acting can be a very physical pursuit. Even at 90 years of age, he can be filming up to 12 hours a day. To keep himself up to the task he takes frequent brisk walks around the sets of *Coronation Street*, plays golf at least once a week and joins regular one hour 'fun fit' sessions every Thursday and Saturday which he says 'gets the heart rate up and raises a sweat'. To maintain mental agility, he plays online chess and Scrabble with his son Linus in the US.

Clearly, Bill's life is anything but sedentary. However, what underpins his desire to be, 'reasonably fit … for filming, meetings, and publicity work', is the third of his philosophies on life after moderation and commonsense, namely, 'enjoyment'. As he says,

The main thing here is that whatever form of exercise you do, you enjoy it. If you don't enjoy it, and it feels like punishment, don't do it. Find an activity that makes you feel good while you are doing it, rather than only when you stop.

People who throw themselves into exercise or extreme diets may be missing out, because if we focus intensely on one thing, we're neglecting something else. We won't be in balance and, when this happens, we tend to lose that bigger, grander, calmer, more peaceful and beautiful sense of wholeness that is ours to enjoy.

In this final chapter of our reflections on the times and life of William 'Bill' Roache, it is important to revisit both a higher purpose and spiritually—this time as it relates to ageing, because it explains and further illustrates his remarkable life journey and even marks a path that others may want to follow.

Martha Crowther's groundbreaking work on *Positive Spirituality—The Forgotten Factor*, for the first time formally linked the science of well-being with spirituality. It described the positive partnerships that exist between health professionals and sacred communities (like Stride for Truth) and how this relationship strengthens interventions that focus on health promotion—an idea that has been well received by the global Third Age community and certainly not lost on Bill Roache. As Crowther noted,

Many gerontologists [have and still do] fail to incorporate the growing body of scientific evidence regarding health, ageing, and spirituality into their conceptual models to promote successful ageing.[3]

Bill's priority is clearly to address this shortcoming by establishing two ideas. Firstly, he takes every opportunity to challenge stereotypes about ageing and secondly, he freely and openly shares the central role of personal spirituality in his own life. These ideas, he argues, are just as important as any practical steps an older person may take to stay well—like socialising, working, or volunteering, diet, exercise, rest and recovery. This all calls into question the misconception that when you age you automatically become redundant; in fact, Bill extols the personal benefits of ageing as,

There are fewer demands upon you in later life, which gives you greater freedom. Your sensitivity and intuition are more honed, and you can rely on them more, as you're less distracted by hurt and upset. You become more relaxed, more aware and a little wiser, and you get closer to your true eternal self.

Being considered redundant as we age shouldn't be acceptable. It's casting aside the wisdom that people—all kinds of people—have acquired

[3] Martha Crowther, et al, Rowe and Kahn's *Model of Successful Aging Revisited: Positive Spirituality—The Forgotten Factor* The Gerontologist, Volume 42, Issue 5, 1 October 2002, pp. 613–620.

throughout their lifetimes. We should benefit from it rather than reject it.

Age UK (Britain's largest charity supporting older people) clearly agree with this. As an organisation they are a national champion for the 'International Care Movement' and the related 'International Learning Movement', which are very old, new ideas.

The modern-day concept started in 1976, when Tokyo-based Shimada Masaharu successfully merged a nursery school and a nursing home, starting a worldwide revolution in thinking about residential care and successful ageing—particularly in Australia, the UK and the US. In Britain, the idea of intergenerational care first came to the public's attention through a two-part Channel 4 television programme called *Old People's Home for 4 Year Olds*, first screened on 25 July 2017. This documented the impact of introducing a pre-school class to a group of older people. The aim was to address the loneliness that many socially isolated people in Britain often experience. However, the experiment had a powerful effect, not only on viewers but the show's children and volunteer retirees alike. The children made new friends and became more confident. Residents were noticeably happier and engaged more with each other.

Age UK points to numerous scientific studies that show that this type of social interaction not only decreases loneliness, but can also delay mental decline, and even lower blood pressure in older populations. According to

Bill's view of the world, what we are observing here are the qualities that define who we are as human beings—'our true nature'. As he further says,

> *To live a long, healthy, and happy life there is one thing we should seek above all else. All the exercise, diets, and lifestyle teachings in the world will only have short-term and minimum effects without this. What is it? Living in a way that is true to our nature. This is profound, and may sound complicated and difficult but, like so many truths, it is simple.*

This statement is a segue to the central role of spirituality in the life of Bill Roache. The relationship between his underlying principles and his open-minded pursuit of peace and happiness have been covered in a previous chapter; however, in bringing this book to a close, we want to relate this aspect of Bill's life specifically to the challenges of ageing as he celebrates his 90th birthday on 25 April 2022—or is that 23 April?

In the preface to *Life and Soul* Bill Roache writes,

> *… I am always looking for the truth, which never changes.*

And on further reflection,

> *We can't change what happens to us, and what happens to us may not always be right but we can change how we respond to it.*

In doing this, all his ideas about flourishing in the Third Age and, in fact, the full sum of his extraordinary times and remarkable life, including an extraordinarily successful acting career, good health and great longevity, can be condensed down to one simple quote. William 'Bill' Roache says these days he, 'worries less and meditates more'—to better understand what he calls, 'his heart, his essence and his true being'.

BIBLIOGRAPHY

Blessed, B., *Absolute Pandemonium: My Louder Than Life Story*, Pan Macmillan, London, 2016.

Copeland, J., Goodfellow, R. and O'Neill, P., *Forty Delicious Years 1974–2014: Murni's Warung Ubud, Bali*, Orchid Press, Hong Kong, 2014.

Copeland, J., Goodfellow, R. and O'Neill, P., *So Many Delicious Years: Murni's Warung Ubud, Bali*, The End Publishing, Auckland, 2021.

Darlington, W.A., *Laurence Olivier*, Morgan Grampian Books, London, 1968.

Egan, S., *50 Years of Coronation Street: The (Very) Unofficial Story*, JR Books, London, 2010.

Glenday, G. and Millward, A., (eds.) *Guinness World Records* (2020), Guinness World Records, London, 2021.

Goodfellow, R. O' Neil, D. and Smith, P., *Saving Face, Losing Face, In Your Face: A Journey into the Western Heart, Mind and Soul*, Butterworth Heinemann, Oxford, 1999.

Goodfellow, R. Copeland, J. and O'Neill, P., *The Pen y Gwryd Hotel: Tales from the Smoke Room*, Gomer, Llandysul, 2016.

Heywood P., *Donald Hughes Headmaster*, Rydal Press, Colwyn Bay, 1970.

Irwin, K., *The Real Coronation Street*, Corgi Books, London, 1970.

Kynaston, D. and Green, F., *Engines of Privilege, Britain's Private School Problem*, Bloomsbury Publishing, London, 2019.

Lawrence, D.H., *Lady Chatterley's Lover*, Penguin, London, 2011. (Originally published in Italy in 1928 and in France in 1929.)

Lawrence, T.E., *Seven Pillars of Wisdom*, Penguin, London, 2008. (Originally published in 1936.)

Maughan, T.L., *The Ancient Druid Order History & Organization,* Lotus Press, London, 1974.

Moran, J., *Armchair Nation: An Intimate History of Britain in Front of the TV*, Profile Books, London, 2013.

Orwell, G., *Selected Essays*, Oxford University Press, Oxford, 2013. (Originally published in 1953.)

Priestland, D., *Merchant, Soldier, Sage: A New History of Power*, Penguin, London, 2013.

Roache, W., *Ken and Me: An Autobiography*, Simon & Schuster, London, 1993.

Roache, W., *Soul on the Street*, Hay House, London, 2008.

Roache, W., *50 Years on The Street: My Life with Ken Barlow*, Mainstream Publishing, Edinburgh, 2010.

Roache, W., *Life and Soul: How to Live a Long and Healthy Life*, Hay House, London, 2018. (Reprinted in 2022.)

Rowe, J.W. and Kahn, R.L., *Successful Aging*, Pantheon, New York, 1998.

Seligman, M.E.P., *Flourish: A Visionary New Understanding of Happiness and Well-being*, Nicholas Brealey Publishing, New York, 2011.

Slade, T., *From a Hard Place to a Rock: Firsthand Accounts of Soldiers of the British Expeditionary Force on the Run in World War Two*, Troubador Publishing, Harborough, 2022.

Stutter, R., *Jonny Kennedy: The Story of the Boy Whose Skin Fell Off*, Tonto Books, Newcastle upon Tyne, 2007.

ABOUT THE AUTHORS

Dr Rob Goodfellow (BA Hons, PhD History) is an Adjunct Fellow and researcher with the Humanitarian and Development Research Initiative (HADRI), Western Sydney University. He lives in Wollongong, New South Wales, Australia.

Jonathan Copeland (LLB Hons) is a freelance photographer and writer who travels extensively searching for the ultimate photo opportunity. He lives mostly in Thailand, England and Bali.

Peter O'Neill OAM (BA Fine Arts) is an arts administrator, writer, and educator with over 40 years' experience in the development and management of art museums and representative organisations within the cultural sector. He lives in Katoomba, The Blue Mountains, Australia.